NEW WRITING / BOOK TALK / NEWS AND REVIEWS

THE RE

No. 37 SPRING 2010

Published by The University of Liverpool School of English.
Supported by:

UNIVERSITY OF
LIVERPOOL

EDITOR   Philip Davis

DEPUTY EDITOR   Sarah Coley
CO-EDITORS   Maura Kennedy
                          Angela Macmillan
                          Eleanor McCann
                          Brian Nellist
                          John Scrivener

NEW YORK EDITOR   Enid Stubin

CONTRIBUTING EDITOR   Les Murray

ADDRESS   The Reader Magazine
                          The Reader Organisation
                          19 Abercromby Square
                          Liverpool L69 7ZG

EMAIL   magazine@thereader.org.uk
WEBSITE   www.thereader.org.uk
BLOG   www.thereaderonline.co.uk

DISTRIBUTION   See p. 128

ISBN 978-0-9558733-6-2

SUBMISSIONS

The Reader genuinely welcomes submissions of poetry, fiction, essays, readings and thought. We publish professional writers and absolute beginners. Send your manuscript with SAE please to:

The Reader Office, 19 Abercromby Square, Liverpool L69 7ZG, UK.

Printed and bound in the European Union by Bell and Bain Ltd, Glasgow

ABOUT THE READER ORGANISATION

Jane Davis, Director, The Reader Organisation

A Reading Revolution!

'People are dying – it is no metaphor – for lack of something real to carry home when day is done.'

Saul Bellow, *Herzog*

We used this quotation in 1997 in the very first issue of *The Reader* magazine. The Reader Organisation didn't exist then, it was just a few friends who wanted to open up the exciting experiences we were having teaching the Literature programme in the Department of Continuing Education at the University of Liverpool. We were running evening and weekend classes for adults willing to read real books from Saul Bellow to Chaucer, via Shakespeare, H. G. Wells and Ann Michaels.

Twelve years on and this magazine, which has been in continuous production ever since, is the voice of an independent charity which is bringing about a Reading Revolution: putting great books in the hands of people who need them.

Amongst other activities, The Reader Organisation is currently delivering 170 weekly read-aloud shared 'Get Into Reading' groups on Merseyside, and supporting the development of many more across the UK and beyond, particularly through our Read to Lead training programme. We work in schools, workplaces, community groups and old people's homes, and a great deal of our work is delivered in partnership with the NHS.

NEWS THIS ISSUE:

Get Into Reading is going Down Under! Our Read to Lead training course has never been in such high demand – the team are off to Melbourne, Australia at the end of March to teach Get Into Reading group facilitation skills!

With the first national **Get Into Reading Conference** being held in Liverpool on 5th March, it looks set that we'll see further developments for the project in 2010. (A report from the conference will be published in issue 38 of The Reader.)

the reader
organisation

UNIVERSITY OF
LIVERPOOL

SCHOOL OF ENGLISH
UNIVERSITY OF LIVERPOOL

TWO-YEAR PART-TIME M.A.
IN READING IN PRACTICE

FOR YOUR DIARY
NEXT ENTRY:
SEPT 2011

*Investigations into the Role of
Literature in Bibliotherapy and Health*

EDITORIAL

GETTING PRETTY ANGRY NOW

Philip Davis

Number twenty-five was a good bus. It regularly took me home from the back of the University, though it doesn't run any more and towards the end became ever less reliable. On one occasion it was very late, and of course getting later and later without end, when one man in the queue starting walking round and round in a tight little circle of his own, muttering to himself: *Getting angry, getting pretty angry now*. I didn't know his exact mental condition or whether he had tenure, but poor fellow, he was a relief to me. I didn't have to *think* it because he was *saying* it, out loud. It is like the man in Les Murray's great poem, 'An Absolutely Ordinary Rainbow' who, more seriously, bursts out crying in a public street amidst amazed onlookers:

> **The man we surround, the man no one approaches**
> **simply weeps, and does not cover it, weeps**
> **not like a child, not like the wind, like a man**
> **and does not declaim it, nor beat his own breast, nor even**
> **sob very loudly – yet the dignity of his weeping**
>
> **holds us back from his space, the hollow he makes**
> **about him...**

I think this man is really the poet himself; his poetry a form of weeping

7

out loud without either the threat of public exposure or the severance of private concealment.

At any rate, *Getting pretty angry now* became a sort of family motto in our house. And it also reminds me how, as a parent, it is so sad when the little ones no longer talk their thoughts out loud when they are playing. The boundaries between within and without get established. The last time I heard my boy's inner voice was when I left him at the school corner, the morning of his eleven-plus secondary-school entry exam, and heard him saying as he turned and walked off from me, repeating it to himself, '*Come* on Ben, *come* on Ben'. Do readers know that poem 'Waking Away' by C Day-Lewis?

I can see
You walking away from me towards the school
With the pathos of a half-fledged thing set free
Into a wilderness, the gait of one
Who finds no path where the path should be.

'I have had worse partings,' says the poet. But 'that hesitant figure', he writes, 'Has something I never quite grasp to convey / About nature's give-and-take':

How selfhood begins with a walking away,
And love is proved in the letting go.

Poetry for me is often about these ruptures. As the years go on, my body walls have got more hardened, also more sensitive to pain, and, of course, I both do and do not want sorrow to break the defences down. 'There is a crust about the impressible parts of men's minds,' wrote John Ruskin in *The Seven Lamps of Architecture*, 'which must be pierced through before they can be touched to the quick; and though we may prick at it in a thousand separate places, we might as well have let it alone if we do not come through somewhere with a deep thrust.'

But anger is an easier relief than the pain of sorrow. I am still effort-lessly good at getting pretty angry now, and yet hardly value the emotion as such. Perhaps it is because I don't want the things that make me angry to exist, and therefore associate the frustrated feeling with what shouldn't be. This is why I was very surprised recently on reading the work of a friend of mine, a musicologist, to find him describing the great opening of the third movement of Mozart's 40th symphony as 'anger'. It has been a key sound for me for more than thirty years now. Winter 1973, I had been talking on the telephone to my old schoolteacher, the novelist Stanley Middleton who died last year. I had been telling him (again and again) how unhappy I was at the university. As he finished comforting me in the old sense of that word ('with strength'), he told me to go and listen immediately to the third movement of the Mozart which I had bought before coming up to college. It meant of course that he was still with me after the call was over, and Middleton was kindly-cunning enough to know that. And as I listened, what the movement meant to me was something like will, creative defiance, breakthrough. But, being music, the feeling didn't have a name or have to have one. My musicologist friend later in his essay describes what he calls anger as really the triggering release of pent-up feelings. That is what I have always wanted: not to have the passions pent-up within, making you passive, making you have them sufferingly; but to be able to express them, *use* them, actively, even in their disadvantage, to *do* some thing or to *make* something.

I am getting pretty angry now about the age of 'cool' we are persuaded into living within. In universities, students reading Hardy's *Mayor of Casterbridge* are persuaded to think more about the history of the corn laws and free trade – proper subjects, things with solid names – than about the dangerously primitive feelings of that raw and awkward man called Henchard. Intellectuals on Radio 4 prefer to talk more about the theme of 'work' in George Eliot's *Silas Marner* than the issues of feeling. This number of *The Reader*, more regular than the buses, seems to us, unashamedly, one of the most emotional yet. See Constantine, McGuinness and Gwyn in particular.

FACE TO FACE

MEET THE POETS

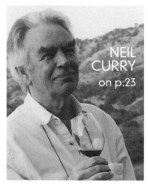

NEIL CURRY on p.23

Favourite place in the world

Holy Island. The island's chief attractions are the Priory and the Castle, but for me it is the North Shore where the gannets dive and Castlehead Rocks where the seals lounge. It is here I feel the presence of Saint Cuthbert, that great Northumbrian Saint for whom I have long felt an affinity. Before me as I write are two of the little fossils known as 'Cuthbert's Beads' and a photograph of Hobthrush, the island where he would go to pray. In my will I ask for my ashes to be scattered there, but am content to wait awhile before that happens.

Which poet would you like to have met?

I would like to have met Elizabeth Bishop and discussed her affinity with landscape. I've long admired her close attention to the details of the immediate world, her precision and depth. Anne Stevenson in an article on Elizabeth Bishop, says Bishop would have gone along with Wordsworth's argument that if you can't say something in everyday words, it is probably not worth saying. I think we can look at complex issues without 'muddying the water', and as part of the writing process, *looking* is the most important facility.

JULIE-ANN ROWELL on p.37

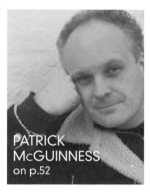

PATRICK McGUINNESS on p.52

Favourite place in the world

Bouillon, the Belgian town where I was brought up. Most of the town is enclosed within the river Semois, which flows around it in the shape of an omega, and leaves the town exactly parallel to, and not much more than a hundred metres from, where it comes in. Between these two points, the river expands to dawdle past, along, under and sometimes through, a medieval castle, thousands of houses, a church, cafés, schools and bridges. Godfrey of Bouillon set out on crusade in 1096 and died in Jerusalem. His name is still invoked as a cautionary tale for those of us who leave.

Which poet would you like to have met?

DAVID SERGEANT on p.73

Shakespeare. Not simply for the greatness of his writing, and not simply out of curiosity, but because I like to think his near-total evasion of biographic history, his apparent indifference to everything but the work in hand (whatever that was), was not just a matter of luck and historic circumstance but the indicator of a high degree of personal sanity. And those who knew him well seem to have thought him a sweet-natured fellow. We'd grab a breakfast of manchet bread and small beer before wandering up to the Globe to check out rehearsals.

ALISON BRACKENBURY on p.79

Favourite place in the world

On the skyline of a hill in Gloucestershire there is a narrow track. It passes the dark ditch of a hill fort, dives into a grassy dip and comes up for air under a line of great beech trees. They were planted over a hundred years ago by a landowner, whose family until recently dominated the County Council, and starved schools and libraries of funds. Yet he loved trees. This is the close of a poem 'Mercombe Wood', to my favourite ridge of scanty earth, and its beeches: 'But as you left high trees to sigh / To crowd tall silver on the eye / Between storm-beaten wheat and sky / I salute you.'

Favourite place in the world

MATT BRYDEN on p.111

The Chapel of St Mary Tory. In Bradford on Avon there's a small mediaeval chapel which pilgrims used as a stop-off on their way to Glastonbury. There's a wooden seat connected to a lectern which holds a heavy Bible, which includes the Apocrypha. You have to sidle into it. The first things I read there were King Solomon's *Proverbs* – 'if sinners entice you, consent thou not' – and the book of Baruch. I was taken aback by its violence. The chapel is the best place in the world to read and think. I'm amazed when I turn the latch and the chapel door actually opens. It's always cold inside, and empty.

RICHARD GWYN

© Rhiannon Gwyn

INSOMNIA

Richard Gwyn

April 2007

My liver has been invaded by a virus. Last December, I was given a year to live, unless a suitable donor is found. Even if I receive a transplant, there are significant dangers: the new liver will not cure me of the viral hepatitis from which I suffer, but will, in turn, become infected. However, a transplant will, in the language of lifespan economics, buy me time.

Along with the diseased liver, I have a creeping madness, gases that gather in my gut and infiltrate the brain. I call it brain fog, but the doctors use another term: *hepatic encephalopathy*. One of the ironies of the condition is that it is almost impossible to say it whilst suffering from it. I wander around the house at night, unable to sleep, speaking to people who are not here. I have a tendency to conjure accomplices from the darkness. And I forget things that are supposed to have happened, while remembering things that probably did not.

One night, I climb to the loft of the house, where my study is located, in search of a cigarette lighter. When I step into the room, swaying under the dual onslaught of sleep deprivation and brain-fog, I am on a mission. I have a cheap lighter in my hand, but it will not suffice, since according to the demented logic of some fleeting obsession, the lighter I am searching for has to be white, and the one in my hand is blue, an aberration. I spot the power lead that connects my laptop to the mains, and it terminates in a rectangular white fixture, which I remove, thinking it might also function as a lighter, and I attempt to light it with the blue one, convinced that the only way to ignite a lighter is with another lighter. I can smell burning plastic, but because of the defect in my cognitive wiring am not immediately able to connect the smell with my own activity, until I realise that the melting fixture is burning my fingers. I am, at that moment, aware of myself as an alien presence, an utter anomaly, a man standing alone in his study having attempted, unsuccessfully, to set fire to a computer, or – which is the same thing – to his memory. The next day I find the blackened remains of the fixture hanging from my desk.

On another occasion, Rhiannon, my fourteen-year-old daughter, discovers me, downstairs in the living-room, trying to stuff a large blue alarm clock with bread. I stand there, in an agony of concentration, wedging a doughy ball into the mechanism with my thumb. I am muttering: *This happens all the time.* At least, this is what my daughter tells me: I have no memory of the event.

I search in vain for any purpose or symbolism behind these temporary losses of reason, or even of basic orientation. Besides, there is little opportunity for reflection of this kind. One evening, Rose, my wife, finds me walking in circles around the bedroom, and I will not respond to any questions from her other than by raising one arm and saying 'No' in a loud voice, flapping one arm like an acolyte of Mussolini, and going off into sudden quieter monologues, barely audible at times, and not consistently in English, but drifting off, on occasion, into other languages, both familiar and invented. Eventually I calm down, but early the next morning Rose cannot wake me from sleep, and has to call emergency services to take me to hospital. I do not recognise her or anybody else, and am in a state of semi-consciousness, which declines, alarmingly for Rose, into semi-coma. I remember nothing at all about that night or the following day. In the Intensive Care unit, a doctor tells Rose that I might not pull through, that it is touch and go. I later discover that only one in five patients survives a coma brought on by encephalopathy.

Before I am fully unconscious, six paramedics and male nurses try to sedate me, and I fight them off with flailing limbs. Rose intercedes, trying to calm me, mutters soothing words, since the efforts of the paramedics are not successful, but she cannot restrain me, my body is out of control and not responding to any instructions. One of the nursing staff thinks I am drunk; Rose informs her pointedly that I haven't drunk alcohol for many years.

But, despite my abstinence, viral hepatitis is destroying my liver, reducing that organ to end-state cirrhosis. As one reliable medical website puts it: 'Liver cirrhosis in the advanced state is characterized by protein wasting, as indicated by the loss of muscle mass, hypoalbuminemia, and an abnormal amino acid profile. The protein wasting condition cirrhosis is associated with a poor prognosis and reduced survival.' Once you've reached this stage, the chips are in.

Cirrhosis of the liver, duodenal ulcers, perforated oesophagus, thrombocytopenia, umbilical and inguinal hernias, ruptured varices;

the prognosis is poor, and the failure of my liver to process proteins causes ammonia to seep to the brain, making me temporarily insane. I can write this in a moment of lucidity, fully aware that another attack is most likely imminent. I might have one now, as I sit writing at my desk, though the chances of this are reduced, apparently, by limiting my intake of protein, while consuming a lot of carbohydrates. They have also given me some more medicine to help with the encephalopathy, which makes a person shit at least three times a day, often more. It accelerates the digestive and execratory process. In this way, the toxins passing through the liver have less time to transform into ammonia and cloud the brain. I avoid madness by shitting more. It makes me smile, the way that the wellbeing of brain and bowels are so movingly interconnected. Get the crap out before it gets to the brain.

Night is falling. From my study window I watch a train pull out from Cardiff Central and I wait, not knowing quite what for. The literature from the hospital Liver Unit tells of 'waiting for the call', yet it does not feel like waiting in any sense that I am familiar with. In waiting for an event which might be life-threatening, and whose outcome is unknown, the waiting becomes *the process*, a seemingly interminable attendance on a Godot whose configuration is as obscure as death itself. My position is precarious: I am on a liver transplant list, but there is no guarantee that an appropriate organ will turn up before my health deteriorates to the point where such a major operation would be unsustainable.

The episodes of encephalopathy are becoming the story of my life. This is what they mean by people becoming their illness, or being defined by it. I am in danger of becoming little more than the embodiment of my illness, and in the meantime I'm going off my trolley, by stages.

Since the onset of brain fog, I have become profoundly distanced from the obstacle course of the world outside this house. This has happened, by stages, almost without my noticing. More accurately, it is as if a protective bubble separated me from the real world and, as I go out less and less, when I do venture into town, or take the dog for a walk in the park, I do not experience life directly, but as if through an invisible intermediary, walking alongside me. Or else I notice things only at the periphery of my vision, witness figures slipping slowly down the knotted rope that sways above an uncharted chasm. The other night, unable to sleep, as always, but incapable also of reading, of watching a DVD, or of writing, I decided, at four in the morning, to visit the all night supermarket in the Bay. I could do the weekly grocery shop, I thought, that would save an extra job, and occupy me for an hour or so. I took the car, and stopping at lights by the bridge across the river, was hailed by a prostitute who was approaching the crossing from my right. A single man, driving around a zone frequently patrolled by members of her profession at such an hour, it was only reasonable of her to assume I might be a potential client. I recognise her: I have seen her before. She has an easier, friendlier manner than many of her colleagues, perhaps she is more confident on account of her good looks, and she is young, though not outrageously so, not like some of the pubescent vampires that haunt the neighbourhood streets. Her face has a certain intelligence about it also, and I think that she reminds me of a woman I once knew, though who knows whether I believed such a terrible cliché at the time or have made it up since; at least her eyes, even from the distance of twenty paces, did not have the frozen-fish glaze of so many of her smacked-out colleagues. Because my gaze meets hers, momentarily, she hurries her pace towards the car, just as the lights change, and I pull away.

Being inside a car, inside a moving object with windows, is a well-worn but precise analogy for the way I was feeling, the protective bubble sensation. Perhaps though, the car exaggerates the sense of desolation I feel when I glimpse the forcing of a smile on the woman's face, a smile that, for that brief instant appears entirely unforced – and again I blame my excitable imagination – as if she has recognised a kindred spirit rather than merely a potential client (why do we hunger so for kindred spirits?) as she hastens her steps towards my car, seconds before I accelerate away, with such an invasive sense of sadness for her, for the riverside wasteland I am driving through, the haze of illuminated rain in my headlamps, for the world my own daughters, safe in their beds, will soon inherit, for my regret for so many wrong moves in the past, for the indecipherable future. When I get to the supermarket, I wander the aisles in a state of suspended but almost crippling despair, selecting goods with placid concentration, there in the almost deserted superstore. I lean heavily on my trolley, with that dull, relentless pain in my side, my feet and ankles swollen with oedema, and by the time I have finished several circuits of the aisles it is seven o'clock and I have spent three hours in this semi-comatose state, here in this tacky emporium of useless goods. When I return home my daughters are finishing their breakfast, preparing to leave for school, and only here, safely back with my loved ones, does the bubble begin to dissolve. I stretch out on the sofa, Bruno the puppy tries to get up with me and wash my face, but I push him away and he lies down on the floor, lifting his head occasionally to try and lick my hand, what goes through a dog's head . . . how I envy him his benign ignorance.

Since writing the above, I have had to stop driving, except in emergencies. I have a tendency to drop off when waiting at traffic-lights, and longer journeys are a nightmare of enforced concentration, gripping the wheel with manic intensity, stretching and flexing my arms and legs, singing out loud, making up ludicrous songs in order to keep awake, although obviously I try to avoid this practice when there are other people in the car. Extraordinary how the insomniac will be overcome by sleep in the most inappropriate settings, but never, or hardly ever, when it is timely, at bed-time for example (how can I begin to describe the effect on me of an innocent phrase like 'bed-time', with all its cosy and infantile connotations of hot-water bottles and teddy bears, with its imposition of a well-rehearsed and ordered normality, or my envy on overhearing a comment such as 'Oh, it's well past his bed-time', as though there was, or ever had been, a time designated specifically for bed, and slumber).

There is no bed-time for the insomniac: you have given up deciding when you should sleep; instead, sleep decides when to take you hostage, often at the most inopportune moments. I have even fallen asleep while giving a lecture, standing, like a horse, and although it was only for the briefest moment, and I don't think (but cannot be sure) that any of the students noticed, or if they did, were kind enough to let it pass, I can only imagine the look on my face when I started from my momentary slumber, looked up in astonishment and fumbled with my notes; poor fool, they must have thought, he's losing it, he probably doesn't know what day it is, he probably doesn't know his own name.

An insomniac is never short of advice from well-meaning friends and relatives. Everyone has experienced difficulty in getting to sleep, and many people feel that this qualifies them to offer advice based on the authority of experience. 'Oh, I have trouble sleeping', they will tell you, and what they mean is that they have struggled from time to time to get to sleep, have tossed and turned for a while, or woken in the night and found it hard to return to their slumber; but essentially these setbacks rarely make a dent on their seven or eight hours of regular sleep. Such people find it impossible to conceive of the extent of disability endured by a serious contender for the World Title, such as myself. Let me make it clear that insomnia is not a question simply of not being able to get to sleep – it is, cumulatively, a massive derangement of the senses, a perpendicular longing, a lacuna within narrative time, a backsliding acceleration into the entrails of night, awaiting the dawn as a mortally injured man might await morphine, in the hope that with the light will come sleep, if only for an hour, or half an hour.

One piece of sound advice from sleep counsellors is to impose a routine on your bed-time habits. Go to bed at a regular time, let's say 11 o'clock, eat carbohydrates an hour or so beforehand (I would favour porridge oats, which has calming properties), bathe my feet in buckets of alternating hot and cold water, five minutes of each, to combat RLS (Restless Legs Syndrome), meditate or practice some relaxing technique such as Qi Gong, take a sleeping potion, either prescription drugs or a strong compound of valerian, play a soothing tape (my favourite one is of waves breaking gently on a sea shore) and lay my head upon the pillow. And yes, I sometimes drop off for twenty minutes or half an hour, if I am lucky. And then I wake with a start, under the temporary illusion that I am utterly refreshed, as if I have slept for eight hours, and I reach for the alarm clock on my bedside table, swear or sigh, turn over, but immediately I know there is little point in even trying: my body has been invaded by several dozen small electric eels, swimming through

"It is humiliating to be so helpless."

the channels of my blood, causing me to twitch and jerk, especially the legs, the arms, and worst of all, this strange sensation of a charge being driven about, wildly, beneath the level of the flesh, like a cattle prod; *it's the virus*, I think, *the virus is taking over, dancing the viral dance.* It knows I am trying to rest, now is its chance to take over completely, and I twist and turn for a while, even take another pill, though not always. I know they have little effect and in any case are not helping the liver, not that that makes a lot of difference, the liver is shot, but I think those pills, temazepam, nitrazepam, dalmane, zopiclone, do add to my general state of confusion, and now I have stopped using them altogether; they contribute also, I suspect, to the outbreaks of encephalopathy, just as helpful to drink a herbal tea as swallow three temazepam, just as ineffective.

I have tried to persevere with the bed-time routine, even when it is so clearly not working, simply because I have run out of other ideas. But lately another element has crept into the equation: dread. I have begun to dread and even fear the allotted hour for slumber. It is not a dramatic sense of terror, more an apprehension that grows with the certainty of failure, borne out by the experience of a thousand sleepless nights. When this dread seeps into the mind and flesh, it becomes impossible even to consider the bed-time routine because the body resists all efforts to relax, to go with the flow, to become at peace with oneself, so essential to the process of sleep, and the restlessness in the limbs then becomes violent and vindictive, as though one's legs and arms have taken on a life of their own and will broach no compromise with sleep. The dread of sleeping is exacerbated by a fear of waking with cramps. These have got steadily worse over the past year. At first they were regular cramps in the calf muscles, but more recently have begun to strike in the feet, and most painfully, the thighs. These thigh cramps are the worst, an agonizing rigidity sets in along the length of the thigh and up onto the groin, causing a sudden paralysis: I wake screaming, an animal yelp that starts in the recesses of sleep and surges into wakefulness, attempt to massage the area vigorously, but almost always, as soon as I begin, the cramps will afflict the other leg, simultaneously, or the same leg, in another place, usually the calf or the foot itself. It is humiliating to be so helpless and in such pain that one cries out in the darkness of one's own home at the dead of night.

Waking in this fashion, night after night, often after only half an hour's sleep, I give up. For long spells, I have resolved not to go to bed at all, and that has worked, after a fashion; I usually drop off around first light. For a while, when still going in to work, I operated in this way. I would spend the night reading and writing in my study, dropping like a stone at sunrise, sleeping until eight or nine in the morning, then getting up and going to my office. But once the cramps have set in, this path too becomes impossible to sustain. Extra salt might help, but doesn't, and is in any case dangerous, considering my medical complications. The doctors have prescribed me quinine, but it has no effect.

Our sense of the passage of time itself accelerates with the passing of time, since each day, week, or year constitutes a smaller percentage of the overall sum of days, weeks, years that have been lived. And yet, of course, as we know, this is a purely subjective experiencing of time, an effect of our having become accustomed to our routines, and the moment we step outside routine, break our quotidian habits, embark on a new adventure, or suffer from chronic insomnia, we experience time differently; we may indeed find that time slows up, and begins to resume a tempo familiar to us from childhood, when the hours would stretch ahead into infinity.

Dipping into Montaigne's *Travel Journal*, an account of a journey the author made to Switzerland in 1580, we find that in a churchyard, at Neufchâteau, the gravestones are inscribed with a peculiar phrase: *Here lies So-and-so, who was dead when time was passing through the year twelve hundred*. That time is itself personified, is conceived of in this fashion, as though it were an active agent, *passing through*, runs in contradiction to the idea, or metaphor, that we are the active agents on a journey *through time*, and this paradox is difficult to sustain, is even shocking, at least to twenty-first century sensibilities.

We are familiar with expressions that rely on the personification of time, such notions as 'Time waits for no one': we accept the cliché without hesitation, just as we can easily conceive of something as a 'waste of time' or try to 'save time' by doing a task in a certain way rather than another (which might involve us wasting even more time): all three expressions are metaphors, of course, but we do not question the notion that, figuratively speaking, we are on a journey, and the idea that Time is On the Move is also a commonplace. Yet the notion that 'the year twelve hundred' might be a static entity, *through which time passes*, is a novel one to me. Perhaps it accurately represents a medieval worldview. If an acceptance of predestination was prevalent among believers at the time, then clearly everything would be mapped out in advance, and although people did not know the outcome of their lives in advance, God did, every hair of the head was numbered, every action had a foreseen consequence, and everyone had their destiny. So the year 1200 came and went, *time passed through*, it followed the course that had been determined for it, by God, and So-and-so died. This conceptualisation of time left nothing

"Yesterday seeps into tomorrow without allowing today to get a foothold."

to chance, or even to choice, since even apparently autonomous decisions were circumscribed by a terrible, all-embracing determinism.

Insomnia allows us a chink in the armour of time. Since we are accustomed to the division of time into identifiable segments, which we measure as hours and days and weeks, we can measure the pace of our passage through time quite conveniently, but once that structure begins to break down, once the notion of 'time passing' over hours and days is exposed as a convenient fiction, everything begins to look rather different.

One of the first things the chronic insomniac notices is an inability to keep track of the days. Since one's life is a continuum of sleeplessness, only snatching rare hours here and there at random times of the day or night, yesterday seeps into tomorrow without allowing today to get a toehold.

Another aspect of insomnia, at least in my case, is *slowness*. Rose has remarked on the fact that my movements, my speech, have slowed considerably over the past few months. We know that cirrhosis causes loss of appetite, fatigue and muscle wastage – this last would account not only for the thinning of my arms while the legs remain swollen with oedema, causing me to resemble a childhood ghost, a character called Mr Wobbly Man, a somewhat tragic figure who used to appear in the Noddy stories of Enid Blyton, and who could not lie down – but it also causes tiredness of the eyes, and a deterioration in my vision, and I am certain that my reactions have slowed. But these are physical phenomena and what I am referring to is *ontological* slowness, slowness of being, slowness of perception, slowness of thought, slowness of speech. Time, it seems has slowed up for me, and the days are not easily measured. I forget things constantly. I recall something as having happened several days earlier, of having met So-and-so in the park during my morning walk, possibly someone real, or a So-and so I have pilfered from my reading of Montaigne or retained from a dream, and my daughters tell me this happened only this morning, and that I have already told them.

Tonight, at around two o'clock, sleepless, I go downstairs, make tea, and settle in front of a television movie in which giant carnivorous spiders are decimating a small mid-western community. I return to the kitchen and swallow a sleeping pill, even though I doubt the wisdom or the efficacy of such a gesture. I take another for good measure, return to the sofa. The spiders are having a ball with the slow-witted inhabitants of what is now Webville, USA. I watch without joy as a citizen is injected with spider venom, wrapped in spider silk and tossed in the county jail by an enterprising arachnid. I switch the television to mute and slide a disk into the CD player, music by a woman whose voice reminds me of drowning birds, but the acuity of emotion is unbearable and after three songs I eject and opt for Bach fugues, played by a Russian pianist with almost pathological exactitude. For a short while, there is no conflict between the need for sleep and the requirement of this music for absolute precision of thought.

Recently, I have begun wearing an expression of stoned incomprehension in public places, and strangers, especially shopkeepers, often assume that I am either drunk or mentally deficient. I fumble for change, unable to coordinate my fingers, my language gets confused, I swear inappropriately as though suffering from Tourette's; knowing that someone is surveying me in the certainty that I must be drunk, I feel frustrated, and even, on occasions, affronted. My family knows that this laboriously slow and slurred conduct is a part of my condition, but for strangers I am simply a moron or a piss-head. The other night I had to go to the garage to buy cigarettes (another habit that is supposed to harm one's ability to sleep): it was around three in the morning and the garage is often quite busy at this time of night. Taxi-drivers re-fuel there, and revellers returning from the bars and night-clubs often congregate, night-birds, assorted lowlife, would-be muggers, miscellaneous criminal and otherwise unsavoury types. The filling-station service counter is staffed at night by an Asian man with a fundamentalist beard; his English is very poor, or maybe it is my language that is incomprehensible to him, because he stares at me with poorly-concealed disgust. I know he thinks I am drunk, and he demonstrates a stubborn refusal to understand my words when I request a certain brand of cigarettes, makes a clicking sound with his tongue, and asks me to repeat myself, which I do, with no success. The man is losing patience, and a queue is forming behind me. I try again, forming the syllables slowly, making sure I do not slur my words. But something goes wrong, whether it is my enunciation, or his lack of

English, or the buzzing of unseen insects on the night air, or the roar of an unseen tsunami rising over Cardiff Bay, or the barrier presented by the reinforced glass panel through which we must speak, I cannot be sure, but I sense we are in a situation of communicative meltdown. As my frustration grows, so too does the muffled sound of complaint from those waiting behind me. I turn to snarl at them; how ridiculous, I am looking for a fight now, I want my cigarettes and everything else has receded into a fog. I am livid that this bastard cannot understand a word I am saying, so I turn around to face a triumvirate of young Somalis in hoodies, no doubt harbingers of random urban retribution, and I envision myself, a few seconds hence, curled in a puddle on the dark tarmac, shielding my head from the blows and kicks that pummel my body, sniffing back blood and snot and tears. Then one of them catches my eye and his face lights up and he flicks back his hood: Hey, man, and he beams at me. I have no idea who he is. You remember me, man? Ahmed, you taught me English. When I first come over. Everything tight wiv you, bro? Need help or something?

I look him in the face: a handsome, smiling boy. He seems concerned, anxious to be of assistance. Sudden clarity: this young man was one of a clutch of Somali child refugees who arrived in the wake of the civil war in 1991. I taught a small class of six, when I worked for the City Council English Language Service, under Ravi Mooneram, all those years ago. He was a good kid, they all were, they had come from hell, they had been bombed by their own Air Force, starved, beaten, in some cases seen their parents murdered, and now here he was in Grangetown, no doubt having benefited from a few years of inadequate education and a further spell at finishing school in the Grangetown Badboy Academy for young offenders, and here, at this miserable filling-station under the persistent drizzle of Welsh rain, years on, he has come to rescue me. His two friends gather round. All three insist on shaking my hand. Hi, I say, nice to meet you Ahmed, after all these years, you think you can help me out here? Blue Camel and some chocolate, any chocolate. My tongue has apparently awakened. I give him a ten pound note and step away from the wretched serving-hole. Sure, man, says Ahmed, and I look away, I've had enough of trying with the hatchet-faced, humourless man at the till, and I hear Ahmed do the business in strangulated Cardiff hip-hop: Gissum camel man, da blue, and a Ga-lax-ee. He insists on counting out all the change and, as I walk away, I wonder at the perversity of a world in which he, whom I helped to speak the language, should have to translate for me.

The work from which this extract was taken, provisionally titled *The Graft* was enabled by a Creative Wales Award from the Arts Council of Wales. The author gratefully acknowledges ACW for its generous support.

POETRY

NEIL CURRY

The Ruin

There are some half a dozen men up there
On the monastery roof, replacing
Tiles and tending to the stonework,
And down here a stack of fresh beams
Waiting to be put in somewhere (*First,*
Cast the beam out of thine own eye.)

What though is it they're trying to prop up?
It stands to reason one day all of this
Will fall, and some astonished survivor,
Shambling by, will wonder what sort of men
Could have built such a thing and who they were
Who lived in what must have been great splendour.

And there will be no one to tell him
That the rich did so to buy themselves time
Out of Purgatory, or that today there are
As many workmen singing and clambering
Over the roof as there are monks inside,
Chanting the hours – the passing hours.

To: Father Ignacio de Madrid, El Monasterio de Santa Maria del Parral, Segovia

That, Ignacio, my friend, was a moment
I will not forget: when you casually
Took down from its shelf a fat vellum tome
And putting it into my hands said that this,
This was Erasmus' own copy of the Works
Of Saint Jerome, and *Mira*, you said, 'Look,'
Pointing to places where he'd crossed out –
Totally obliterated in fact –
Ideas he couldn't go along with.

One idea that I myself find it hard
To go along with is that it's now
Sixty-eight years since you first became
A member of this Order. You were then
Seventeen. Forgive me, but that word
Obliterated comes to mind again.
Damn it though (sorry) you look well enough
On it – except for the state of your teeth;
But then your food is truly awful.

Meeting you has made me hope there just might
Be an after-life – some sort of recompense.
But what? There would surely be some people
Even you wouldn't really want to see.
And how long do you think any of us
Could tolerate having to have all
Our wishes met? And 'a wearisome
Eternity of warbled hymns' was something
Even Milton couldn't bear to think of.

Maybe then, Ignacio, you have it here
Already: the cool of the cloisters,
A clear Castilian sky, pinks and roses,
The fountains and the water-gardens,
And handling books Erasmus himself once held.

(From *Some Letters Never Sent*)

YOUR REGULARS

TURNING INTO BIGGLES

Ian McMillan

As a young lad, I was a completist when it came to reading; I collected Biggles books, buying them with my pocket money, lining them up on my shelves and reading and re-reading them until my mother, looking up from her *Woman's Own*, said to my dad, who was deep in his *Trout and Salmon* magazine, 'he'll end up looking like a Biggles book' to which my dad would reply, in his Oor Wullie way, 'Jings!'.

Actually, I wouldn't have minded turning into a Biggles Book; to me they were (although I didn't articulate this) the highest form of art: they were exciting, they made me laugh, they made me scared to turn the page and desperate to turn the page at the same time, and they made me think about groups of friends and how (and again, I didn't articulate this) they could be the basis of a social and perhaps a political system that could help the world run smoothly, without squeaking or running aground. There was Biggles, and Algy, and Ginger, and Bertie. Around the same time there were other books to collect and line up on the shelf: Just William, with his mates The Outlaws, and I can't have been the only kid who was shocked to find out that Richmal Crompton wasn't a man, and there were the Famous Five: two boys, two girls and a dog. Line them up on that shelf, that endless shelf of remembered childhood books!

I tried to imagine what it would be like if I actually turned into a Biggles book, and one night I had a terrible nightmare that was part scary film and part sound poem where a Biggles puppet with an enormous head the size of the Moon ran around my bedroom shouting BIGGLES in a loud, deep and slow voice. I woke up sweating and laid off the Biggles books for a while, but came back to them eventually like a dieter returning to a guilty pork pie late at night when nobody is looking, only to be betrayed by the crumbs on his pyjamas in the cold and unforgiving light of the next morning. (Yes, I've been there.)

So I guess that's why I've always been a completist, a chap who likes to get hold of all the works of a particular writer, ignoring the fact that some books are just better than others. As a young teenager I became obsessed with the books of John Steinbeck; it started with a Sunday afternoon showing of *The Grapes of Wrath* on BBC2. The film moved me and made me gasp, and the book moved me and made me gasp even more. So I bought the book, in the Heinemann Hardback edition, and I got my mother to cover it with plastic like the books I saw in libraries, so that it would look good. I loved the book but somehow I loved the list of 'other books by John Steinbeck' on the inside page more. Although he wasn't as prolific as Frank Richards, author of the Billy Bunter books, he churned a few out. And I got them all, getting my mother to order them for Christmases and birthdays from the local newsagent who said he got them, somehow, 'from the warehouse…', wherever that was. I imagined a long high room stacked with John Steinbeck books, and an even longer, higher hall, the size (appropriately) of an aircraft hangar, piled with column after column of Biggles.

Some of the Steinbeck books were absolute masterpieces, in my opinion: *East of Eden*, *Of Mice and Men* and of course *The Grapes of Wrath*. But I liked the lesser works: *The Moon is Down*, a melodramatic piece about resistance fighters in Norway; *Cup of Gold*, a forgotten historical novel; *The Wayward Bus*, which detailed a bus journey in which each of the characters was a kind of archetype of American society (there was a character called Pimples who had a skin condition and who broke my heart when he asked the rest of the passengers not to call him Pimples anymore); *Burning Bright*, with its overwrought emotions, and *Travels With Charley*, a memoir about the disillusioned Steinbeck journeying across America in a campervan with a poodle to try and regain his idea of what the country was. They're still there, in my bookcases, and one day I'll return to them, and I'll start with the lesser-known ones and see if they're as good as I remember them. *In Dubious Battle*, anyone? *The Short Reign of Pippin IVth*?

After Steinbeck, I got into Saul Bellow, especially after he won the Nobel Prize, and I still count *Herzog* as one of my favourite books. I liked the way his prose rolled round the page, the way his sentences gleamed and glittered because he'd polished them so much. I had a little bit of a Nobel Prize fixation, and when Alexander Solzhenitsyn won in 1970 I started to collect him. My memory is a little hazy, but I must have been collecting him at the same that I was picking up John Steinbeck, which is an odd thought.

I bought *One Day in the Life of Ivan Denisovich*, his wonderful novella, in a bookshop in Peebles during a visit to my relatives; when I got home I realised that the last fifty pages were just the first fifty pages printed again. To start with I thought it was some kind of post-modern statement of meta-fiction, then I realised it was just an error. It didn't put me off: my shelf-stacking gene burst into life. I bought *Cancer Ward*, which is probably his masterpiece, dealing as it does, in a Wayward Bus kind of way, with a Cancer Ward as a metaphor for Soviet society, and *The Gulag Archipelago* which tells the terrible tale of the Stalinist Terror and the Gulags that anyone who showed just a little bit of dissent was sent to. After that, I got a bit bored with Alexander; maybe it was the translation, maybe it was the vastness of the books. He's still there, though, waiting for me to reclaim him. Maybe I was too young the first time, like I was with Soy Sauce. I'll try him again soon. Mind you, I think I'll try Biggles first...

DAVID
ALMOND

28

INTERVIEW

A VERY GEORDIE GOD

Jane Davis talks to David Almond

What are your earliest memories of books?

I don't remember learning to read. I remember the feel of books, the soft covers of them, even when I was about five years old in reception class. I remember the Headteacher, Miss McShane, opening a cupboard and saying 'You can have one of these', and putting my hand in and taking a book out. I must have been quite little because I was being good, behaving myself. It was maybe *Janet and John*, that kind of reader. I remember the shape of the print and the pictures and the shape of letters and just loving the shapes of it. It was quite a visual thing, I guess and a physical thing. In the same way I remember watching the teacher's chalk. I don't remember the teacher herself but I remember the stick of chalk making movements on the blackboard, seeing the hand move the chalk across the board. It was like magic because it actually meant something. She held the chalk so elegantly. I thought it would break because of the length of stick.

I wonder if modern children will get that sense of connection from a relationship to a keyboard.

That is interesting. Though I think modern children still have what we had. My daughter's eleven now but when she was learning to read I remember her joy at seeing the movement of the hand and the crayon or the pencil.

Do you remember the teacher reading in school? Lots of people of our generation or thereabouts had Friday afternoon stories where they would just read.

No, my main early memory of Primary School is of Plasticine. Making things. I guess I used to like making things. And I remember the severity of some of the teachers and their attitudes to us all. In my last year before Secondary School I went to a Prep School, a private school, which I liked, but all we did was progress papers, maths progress papers and English progress papers, deadly dull. That lasted a year. I have very little memory of being told stories.

What about in your family?

There was lots of story-telling that went on – lots of gossiping – but there wasn't a lot of sitting down and saying 'Now I'll tell you a story'. But there was a lot of people saying, 'I'll tell you now you're older, your Uncle Alban who's in Hong Kong, you know... He'll bring his monkey back this time...' It was that kind of story-telling. We had fairy tales I suppose. And there were lots of stories associated with the church – stories of saints and martyrs, of biblical characters like Moses and Esau, the Fall, the Flood etc, and of Jesus himself, of course. I don't have a strong memory of being read to at bedtime but I know we were read to because I've been told about it. At home, it was more that kind of gossipy, jokey, singy kind of thing that was going on. We had family parties where people sang songs, told jokes, gossiped, reminisced. My Uncle Amos would read poems (he wrote a lot but was never published) and I remember how great it felt to know I had a close relative who wrote – it gave confirmation to my own ambitions.

What's the first book you can remember that got you?

I remember reading a book called *The Grey Pilot* by Angus McVicar, about Bonnie Prince Charlie. He was escaping from the English. It was a great adventure and I remember the sensation of the oars in the water and the landscape of the Uists. Again it's a physical kind of memory, almost like I am Bonnie Prince Charlie being in the boat. There was another book called *The Adventures of Turkey* written by Ray Harris, which I recently found again in a charity shop, an Australian book. I remember my Dad bought it for us as a Christmas present. It was about an Australian boy – his adventures in the outback with his mates.

I remember two books that I had when I was maybe seven or eight, The Wind in the Willows *and* The Tales from the Arabian Nights *and both of them were too old for me, too hard to read on my own.*

I remember that! We had an edition of *Robinson Crusoe* in a red hardback and the print was so small, it was unapproachable and just too hard for me. I thought, I'll never be able to read that and it put me off *Robinson Crusoe* for years. There was a whole series of books like that, hard-backed books with tiny and densely-packed print – and I still have an aversion to dense print. My grandma must have thought I should read *Water Babies* because I remember an edition of *The Water Babies*, and when I think of it I feel quite ill. I think it was the illustrations – there were pictures that seemed quite horrific to me. But then there were books like the King Arthur's stories by Roger Lancelyn Green (*King Arthur and His Knight's of the Round Table*), in a fantastic Puffin edition with illustrations by Lotte Reiniger. I remember reading lots of his books... They're still in print and are wonderful. And Enid Blyton. She does something to children's brains that makes them go 'ping!'

Tell me about English at school as you grew up.

I was a bright kid and when I was young I knew that some teachers and relatives talked of me as being very clever, of being capable of achieving something special. I really began to enjoy reading when I was twelve, that kind of age. But I saw no connection between the books that I read at home and in libraries and the books we did at secondary school. I already knew I wanted to be a writer. I was reading John Wyndham and exploring the library. School on the other hand seemed dry and rather distant. I go to schools now and I think 'Oh, I wish I'd come to this school and I wish I'd had *you* as a teacher'. Secondary school was OK for the first two years but then I began to be disappointed. And I was a big disappointment to everybody! I loved books, I loved writing and I wanted to be a writer, but I didn't feel that I could explore and express that love at school. There were some encouraging teachers there, but the overall ethos was severe and rather forbidding. There's one vivid and important moment I remember, though, when a teacher, for no apparent reason came in and instead of giving the expected lesson, simply read *The Waste Land* to us without any explanation. It was electrifying, and the moment has stayed with me ever since.

Was it a grammar school?

A Catholic grammar school and very aware of its self-esteem as a Catholic Grammar School in the North. It seemed like another world. It's interesting – people tell me all the time that kids don't read any more, and I think 'What are you talking about? *Who* are you talking about?' Because when I was growing up not many of my friends read. I think people are harking back to a time when actually for the bulk of people there wasn't a lot of reading going on. People talk about the great classics that children *used to read*, but when I was growing up, I had no contact with those books at all, Rosemary Sutcliff or *The Hobbit*, C. S. Lewis. And when you look at the riches that schools have now – the rich creative responses to language and the encouragement that's given to kids. It wasn't there.

But still when you went to university and you read English.

I read English and American Literature at East Anglia. This is interesting – I didn't get in the first year I applied because of the reference given by the school, which now seems just breathtaking. I didn't learn this until years later.

Why didn't the school want you to go?

They thought I was a waster and a disappointment! When I applied I had six straight rejections. And of course, because I was the first person in my family to be part of higher education, I didn't know that this was odd or wrong. I went to a college but it didn't work out for me so I applied again to East Anglia and got in right away. The first thing I wrote on there was *Heart of Darkness* and I remember the teacher saying 'This is really good' and I thought 'Bloody Hell!' After all those years of being a disappointment! It was a great course because you could more or less invent your own syllabus. But I knew where I wanted to go. The places I wanted to go to were East Anglia, Sussex, Keele, Warwick.

All the new universities.

New universities with new courses and looking back, though I hadn't formulated it in my head quite like this, coming from my background with my kind of language and my kind of aspirations, I knew that my needs were not being well served in places like Oxford or some of the older universities, even Newcastle.

Were you writing for a long time before you were published?

I was. I was writing through all those years, and the years at school. I always saw myself as a writer. But I was aware that you couldn't actually call yourself a writer until something had happened. After I left university, I kept writing and was published in small magazines, small presses all over the place, and it was like that for fifteen years until *Skellig* came out and then – wallop! – everything changed.

You've probably said this millions of times but where did Skellig *come from?*

I'd been writing for years and had written one novel that was rejected by everybody, and I kept on writing short stories. I wrote a series of stories set in the town where I grew up and it was my territory – they were eventually published as *Counting Stars*. After those stories had gone off to the publisher I was left with a space and out of nowhere *Skellig* just appeared. From the first sentence I knew it was there; the whole thing was just coming out, and I could capture it. I wrote half a page and I knew it was the best thing I'd ever written though I couldn't have planned it. I wrote myself a title page and at that time it was called 'Mr Watson' so I wrote 'Mr Watson, a novel for children' because I knew to my amazement that it was a novel for children. I wrote '35,000 words' and it came out as 35,000 words! I was in the right place. People write dissertations about *Skellig* and about the cleverness of it, and I think, yeah, it is, isn't it!

What are angels?

I think they are imaginary beings that exist in our imagination. I'm often asked when I do talks 'Do you believe in angels?' I always say I believe in imaginary angels. Since the beginning of human time there have been creatures with wings who have been conceived of as visitors who have influenced the way that people think, so to me that's what angels are. They are imaginary beings that suggest there can be some kind of communication between this world and something else, but not necessarily another world. They link the imaginative and real worlds.

Do we get to this somewhere else through our minds, by imagination, instincts or willing it?

I don't believe there's somewhere we'll go to after death. How can you have anything any more extraordinary than this world? I read a book last year called *Run* by Ann Patchett and there's a fantastic passage in that where a priest is dying and he says, 'I've been so wrong, preparing for heaven; maybe this is heaven and the reason we die is because we have to give someone else the space to come and have a look at it'. That's my way of looking at it. The imagination is a huge gift. We can imagine our way into the stars. I don't think there's another world; there's just this world and it's astonishing. That's one of the reasons I resist didactic religion for children because whatever religion they're being involved in, it always says there's a better world than this one.

No. Be here. I love The Divine Comedy *exactly for that reason. It's a man, walking the land, creating an amazing account of what everything is. So even though it's totally within a Catholic Christian tradition, it explodes out of that.*

That's what's needed isn't it? One of the things about religion as it's taught is that it's so reductive. What is heaven? Well, you sit round and you look at God. My daughter cracked that one as soon as she was seven. Hang on, heaven doesn't sound really interesting, does it Dad? Dante makes it seem much more dramatic and worldly.

What happened in your religious life from being in that Catholic School?

Well, I was brought up as a Catholic so there was a strong Catholic community in a little town on Tyneside. I was an altar boy.

I was a Catholic as a child too and it seems to me that it wasn't a spiritual life so much but there was something quite like what you describe in your relationship to plasticine or chalk – something physical. Was that what it was like to be an altar boy?

You had to be trained, I remember being trained in a big gloomy church on Saturday nights. It was cold and you trained your body to do all these things, and you trained your voice to speak the words even though you were never told what the words meant. It's all ritual. The priest is putting his garments on and it has to be tied in the right way, and as he's tying it he's saying his words. And then you're trying to hit the bell at the right time and to make the right movements when you put the tray beneath someone's chin. I was reminded of that recently reading Karen Armstrong's book *A Case for God*. She says religion is not something that you believe but actually it's something that you *do*, that reaches into you as a practice.

I was also in a society called The Legion of Mary; it was a totally barmy organisation: we prayed and did 'good works'. I spent years refusing to write about Catholicism but then I looked back and I thought, my God, you don't want to keep this out because this is wonderful. When *Kit's Wilderness* came out, people referred to the knife-spinning and the game of death, and then I realised it was straight out of Catholicism. It was a Catholic ritual transformed into something else, and the statements fell into Catholic rhythms. Call and response. *'Dominus vobiscum.' 'Et com spirito tuo.'* Choral. Whenever I've written plays I can feel the influence of that; a very powerful and nice thing to have really.

Are you still a Catholic?

No, but I constantly kind of keep ploughing through it. One interesting thing I'm doing at the moment is a mystery play. Durham has commissioned a whole new series: ten new mystery plays. I'm writing Noah and the Flood. That will be performed next May [2010].

Did you read old ones to prepare for it?

I read them afterwards. As soon as I read about the Durham project, I felt immediately that Noah was another story that somehow just seemed to be waiting for me. I jotted down the first few lines and the whole thing jumped into life. It's such a great story. I looked at the Bible story, just to make sure and then wrote it. But after being a Catholic and, you know, and God and all this stuff, to be actually able to have God as a character is great!

Is God angry in your play?

He's angry but he's also got his reasons to be pissed off. 'I gave them everything, nice animals, a nice world, and look at the state they got themselves in. I'll just get rid of them all!' The angels say, 'What, all of them?' 'Ay, all of them. They're a waste of time.' It's a very Geordie God. That's been entertaining to do and very funny. I think in some ways all of my writing is to do with that relationship with Catholicism, with God and belief. I'm trying to work it out.

If I asked you to say two, three, four books that have been shapers…

Hemingway's stories. I remember taking the book out of the bookshelf and sitting down and opening it and reading 'A Clean, Well-Lighted Place', and it opens your eyes. I was fourteen, fifteen and it made me see what you could write. It's a tiny fragment about an old man going to a café in Paris in the middle of the night. And also it was about the language – I thought, it feels like the way *we* talk! *Crime and Punishment* too. I read *Crime and Punishment* when I had flu so I was a bit delusional! I was Raskolnikov. I was nineteen, maybe twenty.

There's a kind of hard and desperate thing about Dostoevsky, which I would find quite difficult to associate with you.

I think it's Raskolnikov's torment, and he's thrusting against the edges of what's possible. He's saying I'm going to try to break through and do something that nobody has ever done before. And then there's *Invisible Cities* by Calvino. I remember the day in Newcastle, going to a bench across the street from the bookshop and opening the book. *Invisible Cities* is a series of stories about cities, which are places of the imagination but also like cities that you could know, Liverpool, Newcastle. It was that blend of the imaginary and the real and it's just a beautiful and a slender book, a very elegant, lovely thing.

You're famous now and – I know you've got to keep earning your living – but you can write what you want. Does that make a difference?

It does because I realise I can do whatever I like but the danger is I could write the most awful book and it would be published. It gives you great opportunities but it also gives you a kind of responsibility to make sure that everything you do is worth doing and that you're doing things that you really believe in. I've just signed to do two books with Penguin, which will be simultaneously adult books and children's books. The first one, *The True Tale of the Monster Billy Dean*, comes out in 2011. I'm really pleased about that because it's a big new step and it feels quite brave. You've got to keep being brave and not getting sloppy.

Write a really big book, you know, big! Do a Dante! I shouldn't even say that in public, that's outrageous.

For Liverpool Reads 2009, we gave away 20,000 copies of David Almond's The Savage through libraries, schools, bookshops, train stations, football club shops and cafes. As one young reader said, 'If I can create the savage, I don't have to be one'.

JULIE-ANN ROWELL

The Uluru Camp

The unfamiliar dark
confounds at first –
we're here for southern stars

and silence
(marred by the freeway —
road-trains dashing for Darwin).

Sand's turning cold, night's
an ice blanket no one quite believes.
Remember heat? No way.

Twelve hundred miles
from the sea,
I feel wildly safe.

The Anangu say,
'Look, see everything', which
in a sense I'm doing.

I need training though
in this desert dust halo
amongst spiny grass, desert oaks,

I've been in a kind of drought.
I recognise it now
this unfamiliar dark.

The Exposition of Waves

Foam whips past us, the wind forces
us to shelter, even the black-backs
fail their perches. You've brought me
to Hell's Mouth where the swell crashes in.

We're hiding, purblind, in the granite beach
and you start to explain the action of waves:
they only give the impression of forward movement,
it's all happening underneath, out of sight.

You talk like a teacher I listen as a student should
to the dynamics of water I've never
cared to understand; your familiar voice like
a father or a brother, the wise old hand.

Holding me, though the wind is onshore,
your fingers tracing my waist. The sea is in my mouth.
I lean back feeling for your weight. It gives,
and for a moment, my balance is gone.

Cleave Church

Crumbling but open to us,
with fox-scented fern and juniper
gathered dead for harvest.
You wanted me to see
the stained-glass window's red.

We held hands at the altar
with a silent congregation:
no cough to remind us,
no baby crying, only dry leaves
hustling up the aisle.

The damp made a face on the wall
opposite the war memorial
where your own surname was listed;
you called it a sign,
but of what you wouldn't say.

I waited for your reviving kiss.
Outside, the crows began
returning to their nests;
black slashes against the red.
You'd turned away your head.

DAVID CONSTANTINE

MEMOIR

David Constantine

y father was not very sure of himself. Often he seemed to be aiming at a right behaviour, and went without the solace of believing he had hit it. What others did naturally and perfectly, he – so he felt – had to aim at the best he could. He came out of childhood without corroboration. All his life he felt he had to make up for bad beginnings.

Aunty Gladys, in a practical womanly way, made up for the failings of the mother. She looked after the father, who didn't deserve it. Dad, who was afraid of his father, attended to his mother very lovingly. He combed her hair, to soothe her; he treated a bad abscess on the back of her neck. It fell to him to make up for Edith, the lost twin, and for the tenderness missing between man and wife. And when he had a family of his own, I believe he was always making up for the parents who had failed him and was aiming at the proper capacity of husband and father; and in his scrupulousness and severe conscience and on the unsteady basis that was his legacy from home he could never be wholly persuaded of his success.

It moved me then and still. I see again and again the face and the gestures of a man doing his best, aiming at his own idea of right behaviour, unsure. Before he died I often felt I should want to speak for him; now it would be truer to say I want to reassure him. Strange that the son should feel he must give the father the corroboration his own father never did give him.

I felt this most whenever he stated something definitely as a general truth. And he quite often did. Like a stammerer driven to have his say, he pushed out at the world in pronouncements whose definiteness was belied by his bearing and his tone of voice. In such sentences he was terribly vulnerable. I used to want to hide my eyes in love and pity from the spectacle of such an opennesss to wounding. Not that he said things that were controversial; often he said things that no one could object to; but altogether it was not what he said but how. The meaning of his sentences lay in their manner. Here was a man trying something out, often nothing very much, with all the confidence he could muster; often not much. Therein their force to trouble and move me lay.

Lines of verse are like that. Their lexical meaning may be only a part, sometimes only a small part, of their whole sense. Indeed, the sense that is borne in the tone and manner of lines of verse may even contradict their lexical meaning.

Once in hospital when I asked him how he was, he shocked me – I was leaning very close and my mother couldn't hear – by answering: 'It couldn't be worse.' That was what he said, but his tone of voice when he said it and the whole set of his life and character were proper for the opposite, as though he were saying what he had said many times before: 'It could be worse.' I feel he thought he was saying that because that, he thought, was the expected and brave thing to say; but what came out was the opposite, nearer the truth. But the whole truth lay in the interplay of the two contradictory sentences, the one said, the one thought.

Long before his first stroke he was talking less and less. He feared that what he wanted to say might not come out right, and that fear embarrassed him. If he was put on the spot by somebody asking him something directly or because he began something and the room fell silent and turned to hear him, then he soon got in a muddle, looked to Mum for help and made the little gestures of self-deprecation which said, 'See what I am like, do your best with me.' This was so for some years before the strokes exonerated him.

We said many times that throughout his final illness, which sometimes they called Alzheimer's and sometimes dementia, he never lost the character he had always had. We meant his gentleness; but his silences, in the end almost continuous, were another such characteristic. He had inclined to silence for many years: in depression, when it is physically hard to speak, the distance between you and any listener seeming too great to cross; in pain with headaches or arthritis of the neck, which suffering he would never talk about; in humility, thinking he had nothing much to say; and also because when Mum was talking, and especially if Aunty Alice and Aunty Gladys were there, with the best will in the world he could not have got a word in edgeways. I once heard her telling him off for not talking enough and he answered mildly that she talked enough for the two of them. But her answer to that was, 'It's a case of having to, isn't it?' She abhorred a silence. When we were all at home, if there was ever a silence at mealtimes or afterwards in the room sitting round, she felt it to be something that had a bad significance. Perhaps she did feel that as he got quieter she had to talk for both of them, to avoid silence. But talking came so naturally to her, she talked so well and with such liveliness, that I doubt if she ever paused and thought it a duty. He would sit there amused and proud – 'She tells a good story, doesn't she?', he would sometimes say – but also, I think, relieved to be let off.

He admired the born talkers. He told me of a man – I think he had only read about him – 'a brilliant speaker', who gave a lecture, 'a brilliant lecture', and being approached after it by one of the audience and asked by this admirer would he give him his notes, he showed a white card on which not a word was written, and gave him that, the blank, the absent safety net, over which, trusting the words would come, he had performed. The story is unlikely, but my father cherished it. That speaker stood above him like a hero in the stars.

He inclined to silence. He never had a language he could quite call his own; then marrying a woman to whom the gift of speech was given in abundance, little by little over the years he began to feel excused; then came his gradual illness when his powers of speech eroded, and her quick and lovely babble covered for him.

But in his last months how she wanted him to talk! She made his speech the marker of his state. So she extolled like proofs from Scripture a couple of perfect sentences he said in hospital. One when she said, 'I love you', leaving him, and he answered, 'I love you too.' Another when Gladys visited and he suddenly said, 'That's my sister.' But most often in her bulletins she would say despondently, 'He doesn't say much. I can't get him to talk.'

This final speechlessness seemed to me in character. It seemed a terminal worsening of what had been his incapacity or inclination all along.

Gladys and Harry finished their schooling, and kept their Salford accents. They were sure of their voices, Gladys especially, she was a great talker, like Mum, like Aunty Alice, in her proper accent. George, the youngest, like Dad, had his schooling halted, but he talked like a man of the world, and he had been all around the world, in high and low society, with the RAF. There was nothing unsure about his voice. But there was about Dad's. When they took him out of school, where he was doing very well, he felt left at a disadvantage, that he must make up by his own efforts. When we were children there was a book of his around the house by C.E.M. Joad, entitled *How to Write, Think and Speak Correctly*. I found a copy in a secondhand shop not long ago. Well-intentioned it may be (Joad was a Fabian socialist), but I can't believe my father could ever have been helped by that book. It hands a language down, from the ruling class to the aspirants. And I want to tell my father that he had no need of it, that he had his own language and needn't go learning theirs. But I can't. I have to admit that he was right in his desire, he did want a better language, he was right to want it and had he had good teachers he would have got it, just as we did, his sons, whose schooling wasn't halted for want of the necessary money gone in fecklessness and drink. He tried to speak correctly, and in the company of men like Uncle Arthur and Uncle Norman, wholly at home in their language, he ended up sound-

"You need a language you can trust yourself to speak in or your voice will not sound like your own."

ing posh. He tried to write correctly, and reached for long and wrong words when the ordinary short ones would have served him best. My mother wrote letters the way she spoke, in her own voice; Dad in what he thought was a better language. The older I got the worse I felt for him. I knew before I could say it that the way he wanted my English to sound – in pieces of grammar-school homework when he tried to help – was wrong, all wrong. I had grounds to resist him in the very reading he was determined I should have and which his own father prevented him from having. I don't see how he could have got to a proper voice. Unlike many he knew what he was missing, but nobody helped him make it up and he hadn't enough resources in his own opinion of himself.

You need a language you can trust yourself to speak in or your voice will not sound like your own and you will always be anxious. I think it was like that for my father. He risked himself entirely whenever he made an assertion in the language he thought better than his native speech and that he was trying to learn. And I think this was one of the strains that either brought his illness on or was compounded by it. The voice in depression is physically hampered and what you utter in it sounds as remote and as little able to engage a fellow human being as shout from under the sea or from off the face of the moon. Both his depression and the impairment of his speech by dementia, the strokes, Alzheimer's or whatever else was doing it to him in his latter years, all seem to have continued that undermining of the confidence of his voice which began when 'Weak Will', his father, took him out of school.

So much he never said. Not just on subjects that embarrassed him, like sex or God, but on himself, his childhood and adolescence, his family, the War. After ECT no doubt he remembered less, but even before it he was never talkative on the subject of himself. Once, seven years before he died – I had climbed Snowdon with my friend Sandiford, it was in the spring of the year in which he would die, he wanted to climb the mountain once with his small son and wanted me with him in case he needed help – I had come back from that and was leaving Mum and Dad in Deganwy and in the minutes before I went for my train suddenly in a rush he came out with things about himself, strange things, more symbolic than factual. I wrote them down. Strange as they are, I trust my own words and believe them.

He was with the Pioneer Corps in the East End, clearing away bomb damage and salvaging what they could. His corporal ordered him to empty a fridge that was full of maggots. He refused. He couldn't do it. The corporal threatened he would be on a charge but still he refused.

Perhaps he had things in him that were unsayable, things it seemed to him he had best not even try to say. Such things as might be represented by the maggots in the fridge in the bombed-out house. So he inclined to silence not only because he didn't trust his voice but because he harboured things he felt ought not to be said; besides, properly worded they would have been unbearable.

It is impertinent of me to speak of giving him corroboration. He was given it constantly by the woman he married. He said to me once that whatever he had achieved in life was thanks to her. She stuck up for him, even against himself. Constantly she persuaded him of what he really was. They wanted to better themselves, which is to say they wanted better lives for their children, they were united in this and since his full-time work, not hers part-time, would be the means, she encouraged him on in it against numerous disappointments. And though in her speech, in her letters and in the childhood memories she wrote when we asked her to, she stuck to her own language, I believe she thought the language he was trying to learn was better than hers or would be one day, for her sons. So in questions of language she deferred to him; but anyone reading their letters, part by her, part by him, would see at a glance that she was at home in her words and he was struggling with his. When they wrote to thank me for the first books I sent them, she deferred to him to write me a word of praise. Then I wished the book undone, to spare us both.

But it seems to me now that his struggle was on my behalf. He lost the vulgar tongue; with the natural raconteurs in it, with Uncle Arthur and Uncle Norman, he could not compete, he could hardly join in, he was sidelined, and anyone who did not love him could think him standoffish. He wasn't in the least. I remember his look when somebody was telling a story – it might be one of the jokers Arthur and Norman, it might be the fluent worldly Uncle George, or Mum, on and on, again and again, however often – his look was like a boy's among grown-ups, wholly admiring, laughing in wonder, with not a hint of jealousy. He was admiring what he did not have, what he could not do, he was between the familiar and the unfamiliar languages, possessed of neither, trying.

What has that got to do with me? His trying has, his trying to write, think and speak correctly – but curse and obliterate the word 'correctly' and set there instead: the truth. Seeking the language for that takes you away from your mother tongue, even if you love its accents heart and soul, it takes you away. I am only doing what he did: trying, not in my mother's tongue, and if I do better than he did it is thanks to him, because he set off, with no help, with no teachers, with no proper guides, into embarrassment, uneasiness, and, in the bad times, far into alienation. So in all the endeavour since I was fifteen to get words to fit, to get them to sound right, to hit the true tone, and especially in my way of going about it, which is to get things wrong, seven times wrong, seventy times wrong, before getting anything anywhere near right, in that procedure through unending trial and error I am like him, he is my predecessor.

After the East End he was in India and there he witnessed an accident. The victim's brains were (his word) 'festooned' all over the road. He was ordered to go and take the details. He refused, he couldn't do it. Five or six months later he was called to court, to testify against the driver they said had caused the accident. Though leaned on heavily by his officer he wouldn't do it. He couldn't swear it was the man and wouldn't.

Demobbed, he was given the usual testimonial but his Commanding Officer then, who had only known him six weeks, added the remark that he talked too much. He was incensed, he protested, but got nowhere with his protest.

This story was among the several he suddenly tipped out as I was leaving after climbing Snowdon with my dying friend. Years later I got his military record from the Ministry of Defence, and there it stood, the official corroboration of a myth: 'A very intelligent man, but talks rather too much.'

The officer can't have meant that my father was garrulous. Rather, I think, that he spoke up when he was not supposed to, that he forgot his subordinate place. He did precisely that by protesting at what his officer said about him, and when the protest got him nowhere he tore his testimonial up.

So this man who had no proper voice spoke up for himself? Yes, he did, and for other people too.

Some early mornings when I lie there thinking about him the paradox is so abrupt it seems unbelievable. This speechless man – as I have almost called him – speaks up for himself against his officers, and thereafter in civilian life does better and better in a job whose essence was talking to people and getting them to talk to one another. Then I think perhaps the problem was mine not his. I watched too much for his vulnerability. I look for the hurt in people. Maybe. But that only confirms our relationship. He is in this writing (as near as I can get) what I felt the two of us to be like with one another. If I write that he

> *"Speaking up was the great victory of a man to whom language did not come easily."*

seemed more vulnerable to me than he did to others (and perhaps even to himself) that is of a kind with my writing in a poem that the Jews on Cheetham Hill were peculiarly lucky when they asked him, as a child, into their houses as their shabbesgoy.

His speaking up, and his acknowledged skill at talking people into arbitration and conciliation, were the great victories of a man to whom language did not come easily.

He never quite believed that he had authority, but felt he ought to have, as the man of the house, and he aimed at it with authoritative sentences, that wrung my heart.

In his work he had authority. When he worked for ACAS [Advisory, Conciliation and Arbitration Service] as a Conciliation Officer and in the few years before he retired when he was manager of the Job Centre in Colwyn Bay people not only liked him (it was hard not to), they also respected him. Surely he knew that? But for many years while we were growing up his self-esteem suffered more setbacks than encouragement. He applied for promotion and didn't get it, and what I remember is my mother's loyal grievance and his self-deprecating look which seemed to say that he sided with the panel, his superiors, who didn't think well enough of him and turned him down. I wonder how many times this actually happened. I remember it as a conjunction of her grievance and his self-deprecation, as though it came round periodically. But this dialectic, with reference to whatever issue, was almost their natural way of being in the world together: her taking his side, sometimes crossly, when he would not himself.

Soon after he died I asked my mother about his depression. We were in their bedroom, she had already given his clothes to the Salvation Army and in a vague way she was opening drawers in the dressing table and finding other odd things of his that were no use now. I wanted to praise him to her by remembering how throughout the years of his illness he always went to work and did his job. She couldn't remember that he had ever been ill like that; she seemed not to know what I meant by the word 'depression'. The most she would concede was that he had been 'a bit quiet' now and then. I began to remind her of the ECT, and then backed off, into my own ideas that it was obvious from her face she did not share.

There are things in my notebooks that I have to trust. Nobody will corroborate them now. I can't myself. All I can do is trust the surviving words.

He had a bad time in the spring of 1981. She said to me then that he had been ill like that for twenty-two years. She could remember the exact moment when it first came on. We were in the church – R. S. Thomas's church – in Aberdaron, at the very tip of the Lleyn, when he left us and went out into the open air, because he felt funny. That was the start of it. She said, in 1981, that in all the years since then he had never been well. In a way she was right: it comes and goes, but the threat and fear of it are always there. But in another way she was wrong: in all those years he had lived his life and done more good than most people. By which I mean that he had effectively denied his illness. In that extraor-

"I rush to affirm a better view of things, as though to say to him, 'It's not that bad'; but he is dead, beyond my comforting, and I'm the one who needs it."

dinary conversation ten years later, when he told me in a rush about his childhood and his time in the army and I prompted him to speak about his illness, he said, 'My life was ruined by valium and a poor upbringing'; but though it shocked me then and distresses me even more when I think about it now, in my heart I don't believe he thought his life was ruined. He never said anything like that – not to me at least – before or ever again. So I rush to affirm a better view of things, as though to say to him, 'It's not that bad, see what you did in the life you say was ruined'; but he is dead, beyond my comforting, and I'm the one who needs it.

I wanted to praise him to my mother by saying he was ill, he was clinically depressed, and hardly ever had a day off work, always turned in, looking smart, and did his job, which was helping other people, but she didn't need that praise, she was elsewhere, and remained there, in the husband and wife place that wants nobody else, not even the sons. So I write it for myself because I am dwelling on him as a brave man who did well at things he had to struggle at. I have to contradict her.

Once he dropped me at Aber so I could climb the Falls and walk back to Deganwy over the hills. He had to visit a firm, to sort their problems out, and he dropped me off on the way, so I could have a walk. He couldn't speak, he was utterly in the grip of it, and when he left me he had to go and meet people and talk and get them to talk. Another time Helen and I were at the cottage under Moel Eilio and he came to stay the night because he was in that area, visiting firms. Again, when he came in he could barely speak. In his suit, with his briefcase, he was in hell, remote as hell, in the deep deep suffering and solitary confinement of that illness. We had been out on Moel Eilio or the Elephant Mountain picking whortle-berries and Helen had made a pie of them, for a treat when he came in. Those two occasions are representative. First because he was in hell but in the company of people who, setting off to climb the Falls or come back from getting whortleberries on sunny Eilio, were as near to paradise as people ever are on earth. That's how apart a man in depression is. And secondly because, knowing we loved him, he let himself lapse into the silence whose deadly pull his job must force him to resist all day.

My mother told me in the spring of 1981 that he had come home and burst into tears. That was in Deganwy, soon after his retirement. I remembered that it had happened before, perhaps near the beginning of the twenty-two years she was so precise about, in Salford, and I was there at the door with Gran when he rang the bell. But why would he ring? She opened the door, he stood on the step and wept. 'Bernard,' she said, 'whatever's the matter?' and brought him in. Why did he ring? Why didn't he use his key? Perhaps he hadn't the strength of body and soul to let himself in. He had got that far, to somewhere kind to him, and he could do no more, except ask to be let in. If I am right in my idea that he was a man all the time aiming, unconfidently, at things a man ought to be and do, then weeping on the doorstep will have seemed to him disgraceful. I imagine him doing his job, all day speaking and answering when necessary, all the while in the hell of utter loneliness, all the while nearly saying so: nearly saying: 'See how far from you all I am', but not, not saying it, but doing and speaking the part so well they did not notice, and by main force of will then reaching home. It was his just deserts, being largely of his own making, that the house and home he reached were unconditionally kind to him and that in it there was no suggestion, not the least shadow of one, that collapse when you cannot hold up any longer is disgraceful.

In the East End during the Blitz surely he saw worse things than maggots in a fridge? Perhaps those worse things suddenly gathered there. One image held them all. Then at that moment he and the cor-poral were on different levels of life. He was looking into the eyes of horror, and whether the corporal put him on a charge or not mattered very little in comparison.

He was not squeamish about things at home. He bathed the foul abscess on his mother's neck. Mum always said he was the most reli-able in any crisis, when somebody had an accident and there was a lot of blood. When Gran died at home he saw to everything very briskly, to spare her daughter. So perhaps the maggots in the fridge and then the brains on the road in India were occasions when the horror of life – which I believe he quite often looked into, the first time being when his twin sister burned to death at the age of three – suddenly gathered and opposed him, so that he disregarded his position, which was to obey orders, because his own nightmare was a greater authority.

After the War, which is to say throughout my lifetime with him, I don't know that he met with things like that again. Instead, when he was clear of them and was doing well in his capacity as husband and father, depression fetched them back. I don't mean in their particularities. Depression, when it comes, lets you know that you are living on unstable ground, on a fault-line through unstable ground, over a welter of things that have been banished from or have never seen and seem to want to force themselves into the light of the sun. Depression is the fissure through which they rise. So that funny feeling in Aberdaron church and the bewilderment on public transport after ECT and the remoteness and solitary confinement at work and in the family and the occasional collapses into tears: these are brushes with the horror of life, little insights into it, into the dread of meaninglessness and alienation, and the fact that they came over him when real occasions like the maggots were in the past and the death of his twin sister Edith was dead and buried beyond memory, is only an irony in the nature of depression. I suppose the past, biding its time, emerged into the daylight when he thought he was rid of it, when the struggle for a decent living was won, when his sons were doing well. He didn't know why, amid his blessings and achievements, he should be ill and none of his many doctors did either. Altogether the doctors he went to were ignorant and helpless. He tried out pills for them, one kind after another. They gave him ECT, which impaired his memory. In sum their treatment only fuddled him.

He had his own idea of what a father should be like, and he lived up to it. Countering the model of his own father he made us toys, he took us for walks, he took us cycling, fishing, sledging, flying kites and aeroplanes. He taught us to raise our caps to ladies and stand up for them and the elderly on buses, he taught us how to bat and how to bowl. Year by year for his own poor childhood Christmases – uncelebrated, bare of gifts – ever more lavishly and with a magician's imagination he made it up to us. He sacrificed the centre of his lawn to us every Bonfire Night.

He mended shoes, laid crazy-paving, dug and concreted a paddling pool (that hedgehogs came to drink at), painted, decorated, spent hours up ladders, hours in the garden over roses, strawberries, raspberries and blackcurrants. Of many of these occupations he would say, 'There's an art in it', and meant, 'which I don't have.' If you ever commended him, he would answer, 'Jack of all trades', and add 'and master of none.' I bless him for the shed, the last, the dangerous knife, the smell of paring leather, the shapes of sole and heel. I came out of childhood thinking: a father does things, there is nothing a father cannot do. Now I know (or think I know) that he was modelling himself on his own idea of the family man, doing his best, thinking all the while there's an art in this that I don't have have but will go after nevertheless.

He went in among all kinds and classes of people and into all sorts of conditions and circumstances. For a start, the family he was born into he didn't, unlike his brothers, seek as speedily as possible to get out of but took it upon himself to be the one its failures and humiliations affected most. He tended his mother, he carried on looking after her and witnessing her disgrace.

He was in the Blitz on the Mile End Road, he was a military policeman in Karachi, he worked in the roughest employment exchange in Salford, by the docks where the men came off the ships and violently demanded their rights. He worked. As a boy, among other jobs he made ice cream. The pay was a shilling, he gave his mother eleven of the pence. From messenger boy in the Post Office to manager of the Job Centre in Colwyn Bay he was fifty years working. Along the way he did extra jobs – in an electro-plating factory (where the fumes made him sick) or as a clubman in the dark evenings on a bicycle from door to door – to add to his regular income and better his family's prospects. With ACAS and when he ran the Job Centre he saw every kind of trade and occupation around Manchester and in North Wales. He was everywhere, among all sorts of people, and saw the hundreds of different ways of managing and coming to grief in the real world. And by people of every kind and class he was loved and honoured. This man, my father, who mixed so bravely with the real world and whom I come trailing after in the wish and responsibility to do the same, why should I feel I have to write and reassure him? Only that I think he never looked around him at our lives and gave himself the credit due.

26 April 1998

POETRY

PATRICK McGUINNESS

My Mother

How I think about her now is how
a thought is said to cross the mind:
like a bird's shadow as it flies,
dragging its span in darkness along the ground.

L'Air du Temps

Tracing her perfume, link by link of vapour,
through the crowd to where she's not, to where
her scent expends itself in air,
I pass through as if the ghost was me, not her.

French

Teaching it to my children I think of it now as my mother's
tongue if not, any more, my mother-tongue. It's freighted
with a kind of loss; hers, mine, and what she lost
as she passed it on to me, continents away from where she started:
shot through with gaps, mothballed and moth-
eaten at once, the smell of preservation neck and neck
with the smell of death. Lying for years in the cellar,
it fattened up, grew milky, slow, echoed in my mouth
as in a tunnel of its own disuse.
                             Then, like drinking
from the source, came our annual summers in Bouillon,
where our Belgitude rose up in us like the damp
behind the wallpaper in the house that stayed unused
nine months out of twelve: its empty rooms,
lost cupboards, the stored-up junk piled up so long
that each forgotten item now dovetailed into the next,
a perfect carpentry of abandonment; it was the tongue
and groove of unused words, life in suspension: ready to rise
again like dust in the backdraft from a closing door.

There's something in it when I use it here brings back
those moments when, mid-play, I'd nip indoors for a piss
or for a sandwich and when I came back out the other
children were all gone, the courtyard empty, the toys
back in their boxes and the sky already crossed with evening;
brings back the knowledge, always wrong but always knowledge,
that there would never be another time than this,
this ending-tainted perpetuity.

Now my children taste it,
the empty-courtyard French I used to speak;
they push their tongues along the language
and as I hear their words snag I hear my own again
and wake from that recurrent dream in which
I'm always waking up, and break off that aborted
first line of my story which I'm always starting:
that I'm much younger and still Belgian.

PATRICK McGUINNESS

FICTION

THE LAST HUNDRED DAYS

Patrick McGuinness

'And yet, the ways we miss our life are life'
– Randall Jarrell

I n 1980s Romania boredom was a state of extremity. There was nothing neutral about it: it strung you out and stretched you; it tugged away at the bottom of your day like shingle scraping at a boat's hull. In the West we've always thought of boredom as slack time, life's lift music sliding off the ear. Totalitarian boredom is different. It's a state of expectation already heavy with its own disappointment, the event and its anticipation braided together in a continuous loop of tension and anti-climax.

You saw it all day long in the food queues as tins of North Korean pilchards, bottles of rock-bottom Yugoslav Sliwowitz or loaves of potato-flour bread reached the shops. People stood, in sub-zero temperatures or in unbearable heat, and waited. Eyes blank, bodies numb, they shuffled step-by-step towards the queue's beginning. No-one knew how much there was of anything. Often you didn't even know what there was. You could queue for four hours only for everything to run out just as you reached the counter. Some forgot what they were waiting for, or couldn't recognise it when they got it. You came for bread and got Yugo rotgut; the alcoholics jittered for their rotgut and got pilchards or shoe polish, and it wasn't by taste that you could tell them apart. Sometimes the object of the queue changed mid-way through: a meat queue became a queue for Chinese basketball shoes; Israeli oranges segued into disposable cameras from East

Germany. It didn't matter – whatever it was, you bought it. Financial exchange was just a preliminary; within hours, the networks of barter and black-marketeering would be vibrating with fresh commodities.

It was impossible to predict which staple would suddenly become a scarcity, which humdrum basic would be transformed into a luxury. Even the dead felt the pinch. Since the gargantuan building projects had begun in the early 1980s, marble and stone were requisitioned by the state for façade work and interior design. In the cemeteries the graves were marked out with wooden planks, table-legs, chairs, even broomsticks. Ceausescu's new Palace of the People could be measured not just in square metres but in gravestones. It was surreal, or would have been were it not the only reality available.

I had arrived full of the kind of optimism that, in retrospect, I recognise as a sure sign that things would go wrong, and badly. Not for me, for I was a passer-by; or, more exactly, a passer-through. Things happened around me, over me, even across me, but never to me. Even when I was there, in the thick of it, during those last hundred days.

To step onto the half-empty plane that mid-April day was already to step back in time. Even at Heathrow, with the flights landing and taking off all around us and London proliferating in the distance, our plane had become a capsule of its destination and its epoch. Both felt further away than the three and a half hours it took to fly to Bucharest.

I was still in my suit. I had had no time to change, much less go back to the house before catching my flight. I had attended the funeral with my suitcase and hand luggage, which I left in the crematorium lobby during the service. I hadn't meant to upstage him – there was room for only one departure that day – but that was how it all fell together: my new job, the new country, unalterable plane tickets. 'It's not every day you bury your father', someone had said to me by way of reproach. *No, but if like me you spent every day wishing you could, the event itself was bound to have its complicated side.* Of course, that's not what I replied. I just nodded and watched them all pretending to pray, straining for that faraway look, something in themselves to help them say, later, how they'd levelled with death this afternoon, and hadn't erred into thinking about dinner or tonight's TV.

The flat that awaited me was surprising in its size and elegance: the whole second floor of a large 19th century house on Aleea Alexandru, in Herastrau, a part of old Bucharest which remained for now untouched by Ceausescu's great 'modernisation' project. This was where Party apparatchiks, diplomats and foreigners lived. All over town churches were being torn down, old streets obliterated and concreted over. Here it was possible to imagine otherwise, though the noise of building and demolition was always there.

On the front door the previous occupant's name was still on a card in a small metal frame: 'Belanger, Dr F.' Mine was written on an envelope containing a key and a note inviting me to make free with whatever goods remained. The phone was connected, the fridge and cupboards stocked. The wardrobes were full of clothes that fitted, and there were books and records I might have bought myself, along with a video recorder and TV. My predecessor must have left in a hurry.

It was six pm. I went to the fridge for one of Belanger's beers, then out onto the balcony. The tiles were hot underfoot and I settled into an armchair of frayed wicker to watch the street below.

I must have slumbered because when the doorbell rang it was fully dark and the tiles were cold. In the darkness of the flat, a phone I had not yet seen rang three times, paused, then rang again. I lifted the heavy bakelite receiver but the caller had gone. There was a tiny click and then the flat tone of a dead line.

The electricity across town had cut out, though here in Herastrau we were spared the worst of the power stoppages. I was conscious, now that traffic had died down, of a constant noise of clattering metal, drilling and thrumming engines. I stumbled through the darkness, unable to find the light switches, only gauging the position of the front door from the repeated buzzing.

At the door stood a short, overweight, lopsidedly upright man with a face full of mischief and an alcohol flush. I knew who he was, though I had never seen him before. I motioned him in with an easeful proprietorial gesture that suggested I had been here longer than a few hours. But I felt at home in Belanger's flat, and even his things, foreign as they were, seemed to confirm me.

'Leo O'Heix. Remember me?', said the new arrival with a mock-military click of the heels, a rolled-up copy of Scinteia, the Party newspaper, in his jacket pocket. He jabbed a hand at me but elbowed past before I could shake it. 'From the interview?'

I had not been to any interview. I had applied for a dozen postings, been interviewed for six, and failed to get any. When the Romania job came up I was too disheartened to turn up to the interview. When, two days later, I received a letter 'pleased to inform' me I had been selected, I thought it was a joke. When the visa followed a week later I realised it wasn't. 'You were probably the only applicant – everyone else got the good postings and you got what was left', my father had said. He was unable to piss or shit or even eat unaided by then, but he could still rouse himself for the occasional sally of malice. But in this case, and for the first time in his life, he was giving me too much credit: I had dramatically improved my employability by not even attending.

Nursing my father through the last months was a test of endurance for both of us. I wheeled him through the wards as he fulminated about bad spelling, poor grammar, grocer's apostrophes on the laminated hospital noticeboards. The habits of work remained with him: twenty years in Fleet street, he had manned the newspapers' hot metal printing presses, setting the pages by hand, learning his trade and learning, as he went, a way with words that a less unhappy man would have put to better use than he did. When they sacked him, along with six thousand other print workers three years before, he stood on picket lines for a few weeks and threw bricks at police cars before one morning going back to work in a reinforced strikebreaker bus, its windows painted over and layered with wire mesh, protected by one of the new private security firms.

As he died slowly we kept reconciliation at bay by talking only about trivia. In those last few days of delirium he asked for her, my mother – complained she wasn't here to visit him. Even at the end he was still finding new ways to be angry. The doctor was baffled by the way he fought the illness inch by inch, holding his ground when by rights the cancer should have claimed him months before: 'trench warfare' he called it. I knew what it was that kept my father going: anger.

Leo turned on the lights and made for the drinks cabinet with a manner yet more proprietorial than my own. Pouring a glass of gin, topping it off with a symbolic shake of the tonic bottle, he went to the freezer and tipped in a couple of ice cubes. This done, he sat on the sofa, crossed his legs, and looked up at me expectantly. My move.

Leo wore a sweaty flat cap that looked screwed on, leaving circles of red indented grooves on his forehead, and his skin was the texture of multiply-resurfaced tarmac. His trousers were the colour of blotchy mushrooms, and though his legs were the same length, theirs were not. His shirt was that special of streaky grey that comes from having started out white and spent years sharing washing machines with blue underpants.

Still dozy, I was finding it hard to compose myself. But composure was unnecessary: before I could say anything, Leo finished his drink and leapt up.

'We're going for dinner'.

He pushed me out of the flat and into the hallway. The phone rang behind me, but Leo had already shut the door.

'There's a few things you'll need to know…' Leo begins, sloshing the wine around his mouth and swallowing it back hard. He abandons his sentence and looks me up and down for the first time.

'You look like someone who thought they could travel light but who's already missing his baggage.'

I tell him I'm tired, jetlagged by far more than the two hours time difference between Romania and Britain; that I'm sitting in an improbable restaurant in the half-lit capital of a police state with a jittery drunk; that I'm here because I got a job I never applied for after an interview I never went to; that under the circumstances my baggage is all I've got to hold on to in these unreal times.

'Enough about me. Tell me something about yourself...' Leo has said nothing about himself. 'You were most impressive at interview. Ticked all the boxes.'

'Very funny – tell me, how much of a disadvantage did not turning up put me at?'

'Well, I pride myself on being able to see beyond first impressions... Professor Ionescu's looking forward to meeting you too. We think we've appointed the right person for the job. Someone who'll, er... grow into it. You'll notice too that we've taken the liberty of adding BA to your name: Bachelor of Arts. A welcome present from me,' Leo pushes a degree certificate across the table, an ornate, multiply stamped and signed piece of parchment with a blot of sealing wax and a ribbon. First Class Honours, *Summa cum Laude*. 'Mind you, if you want a PhD you'll have to pay for it like everyone else.'

Leo shrugs and laughs – he's already onto the next thing, ready to give me the lowdown. 'And believe me, it's low'. His joke falls flat (is it a joke?), but he is undeterred. He begins the pep-talk he has given many time before. Dozens of people have passed through before me, but none of them stuck it out beyond a few weeks. Only Belanger had looked as if he'd stay the course, but Leo does not talk about Belanger.

Leo explains, Leo contextualises and embroiders. There are things to exaggerate and things to underplay. After a few months here, it will amount to the same thing: life in a police state magnifies the small mercies that it leaves alone until they become disproportionate to their significance; at the same time it banalises the worst travesties into mere routine.

Our waiter, itching with solicitousness, comes to ask – an unheard-of enquiry in the Eastern Bloc – 'if all is delicious?' Since we have not ordered yet, this is certainly a good time to enquire. His eye is on the packet of Kent on the table.

Leo replies *Da, multumesc*, yes, all is very delicious.

'These new-fangled ways...' says Leo, referring to the man's inexpert ministrations, 'asking you if your food's good, telling you to enjoy your meal. I preferred it when they slammed the grub on the table and went off scratching their arses... It's something they've picked up recently from foreign television. When I first arrived in Bucharest, I came here for lunch and one of the cleaning ladies was clipping her toenails on the carpet. That was old Romania, Ah! The old days… now it's all Hi! My name is Nicolae and I'm your waiter for the evening…' Leo's American accent is terrible. 'I blame *Dynasty* – they've started showing an episode twice a week. A way of using up a quarter of the three hours of nightly TV. It's supposed to make Romanians disgusted by capitalist excess but all it does is give them things to aspire to.'

He motions the waiter to take our order: the house speciality, 'Pork Jewish Style', a dish in which a whole continent's unthinking anti-Semitism is summarised.

Leo eats like a toddler, cutting pieces of food with his knife and skewering them to the end of the fork with his fingers, before changing hands and loading the food into his mouth. In between mouthfuls, the fork stays in his fist which he stretches right back behind his right shoulder, far from his body, like tennis player waiting to deliver a forehand.

'This is a country where 50 per cent of the population is watching the other 50 per cent. And then they swap over.'

I listen to his bad jokes and already I know they aren't really jokes at all, just ways of approaching the truth at a less painful or depressing angle, like walking sideways in the teeth of a vicious wind. I eat the food and drink the wine as Leo describes a world of suspicion and intrigue in which he is happy, stimulated, fulfilled. The place suits him, not because it resembles him but because he is so far in excess of it.

But most of all, he loves it: 'It's all here, love, intimacy, human fellowship. You just need to adapt to the circumstances' says Leo, 'It's a bit of a grey area to be honest. Actually, I might as well tell you the truth: it's all grey area round here', he gestures at the world outside Capsia as if it is a correlative of the moral universe we now live in. He motions for a 3rd bottle of Pinot noir. I wonder if they have aspirin in Romania. Christ, I think, what a start.

Sitting in Capsia that night I felt two things, two sensations that seemed at odds, but which took me to extremes of myself: a sense of the world closing in, tightening up, an almost physical sensation of claustration; and something else, exhilaration, a feeling for the possible, something expanding around me as I looked out at that empty square. It was as if the agoraphobia the new city was designed to induce, and the political system it existed to make concrete, was translating itself inwards, becoming an intensive inner space. The way an atom could be split to open out a limitless vista of inverted energy, so now, in the midst of constraint and limitation, my life seemed full of possibility. I had been here only a few hours; nothing had prepared me for any of this. But I felt ready.

Ready for what, however, I had no idea.

The first thing I learned, and I learned it from Leo, was to separate people from what they did. People existed in a realm apart from their actions: this was the only way to maintain friendships in a police state. When Rodica, the faculty secretary, opened our offices for the police to search our things and copy our papers, or the landlady let them into my flat, I said nothing. I knew they knew I knew, and it changed nothing.

For all the grotesqueness and brutality, it was normality that defined our relations: the human capacity to accommodate ourselves to our conditions, not the duplicity and corruption that underpinned them. This was also our greatest drawback – the routinization of want, sorrow, repression, until they became invisible, until they numbed you even to atrocity.

I slept late and woke in sunlight so hot the blood bubbled inside my eyelids. My first morning was given over to residency formalities at the Ministry of the Interior. The building dominated a roundabout so large it outscaled even the cranes and diggers that stalked the city's streets like Meccano monsters. A few old buildings stood across the way, precarious for all their seniority. Perhaps their foundations already tingled with intimations of demolition: in six weeks they would be gone. From the outside, the ministry was boxy and grey, its only ornament a stucco Party crest. As an interior space, it was barely comprehensible. I remembered those posters by Escher that decorated student walls: physically impossible architecture and abyssal interiors; staircases that tapered into a void, or twisted back into themselves; doors that opened onto doors; balconies that overlooked the inside of another room that gave onto a balcony that overlooked the inside of another room.... There were vast desks with nothing on them except for telephones, ashtrays and blank paper; voices loud enough to startle but too faint to understand; unattributable footsteps that got closer but never materialised into presence, then sudden arrivals which made no sound. The rustle of unseen activity was everywhere, like the scratching of insects in darkness. Kafka's *The Castle* came to mind, a book I had not read but that fell into that category of literature that culture reads on your behalf and deposits somewhere inside you. So I imagined Kafka's castle.

After an hour's wait, a man appeared, blinking and smelling of basements. I filled in the forms, leaving only the 'Next of Kin' box empty. I had looked forward to the ceremony of leaving it blank, the cleanness of it. 'No kin' I said, 'no next'; but he insisted I write something. There were no blank forms blank in this country. I wrote Leo's name.

MICHAEL SCHMIDT

© Benedict Schmidt

THE POET ON HIS WORK

ON 'ALSO, POOR YORICK'

Michael Schmidt

I n 1985 C.H. Sisson sent me his translation of Andreas Gryphius's 'Gedancken über den Kirchhoff und Ruhestädte der Verstorbenen', first published in Breslau 1657. Gryphius's father was a Lutheran pastor, and the poet was born in Glogau, Silesia, a town recently ruined by fire. When he was two the Thirty Years' War began. His early sonnets, Sisson remarks, were about 'this world of blood, pillage, fire, rape, famine'. He was well educated and well travelled. He spent his last years back in Glogau as an official and there composed 'Gedancken'. I published it in full – fifty eight-line stanzas – as 'Thoughts on the Churchyard and the Resting-places of the Dead' in *PN Review* 44 twenty-five years ago.

This merciless poem could hardly be further from Gray's 'Elegy'. Gryphius imagines the final judgement and the opening of the graves. In the fifteenth stanza he writes:

God help me. Coffins open wide,
I see the bodies in them move.
The army of the once alive
Begins to exercise anew.
I find myself surrounded by
A host death has deprived of power
A spectacle which forces showers
Of burning tears from my blank eyes.

He moves from this terror, through gloating at the fleshless, worm-riddled fate of his foes (less a mournful *ubi sunt* than a wry *ibi sunt*, with them reduced to burst skulls and disconnected bones), to a sense of his own mortality (Larkin's 'Well, we shall find out' from'The Old Fools') and, at last, to the promise of eternal life. Transfiguration in the poem is less real, less credible, than rank mortality and decomposition.

The Jacobean, baroque, grim wisdom of this poem is a sophistication of the sinister churchyard in Elsinore where Hamlet handles Yorick's skull. Gryphius's poem has stayed with me, both as a vision of mortality and as a teasing, unlikely promise of resurrection, a theme that fascinates the reluctant Anglican in me and the pagan lover of Ovid and the metamorphoses of classical legend. One of my favourite poems by C.H. Sisson is 'Metamorphoses': in it the classical stories are not driven out by Christ, as in Milton's 'On the Morning of Christ's Nativity', but redeemed. Sisson writes, 'The metamorphosis of all/Or he was nothing but a child...' And so it is. Perhaps.

Gryphius, Sisson and of course Shakespeare are behind the poem 'Also, Poor Yorick'. Some readers will spot David Beckham, from the time of the last World Cup, in ghostly form. Years ago I saw a Pre-Raphaelite painting of a swarm of souls in white gowns clouding up into the heavens on their way to salvation. It was a huge, poor painting but a memorable vision that also informs the poem. The little jet of Latin is conventional: I first read the epitaph on a gravestone pavement in Toledo in my late teens: *Hic iacet cinis pulvis nihil*, anonymous. There is a painting by a colonial Mexican artist in the gallery of the Viceregency in Mexico City showing Christ with a spear or arrow in his side upon which a burning phoenix perches. Sebastian can't be far away (he never is). In my poem the arrival of Hamlet, too equivocal to believe, too self-engrossed, is not a Stoppard gesture. In the larger drama it is Yorick who shows the way and poor Hamlet who has the walk-on part.

One among the ghostly presences in the poem is that of my dear editor Peter Sansom who wisely removed an effortful scene-setting first stanza and pushed the reader in in *medias res* as it were, at the deep end, where he or she may choose to swim, or sink. The book of ballads is *Tottel's Miscellany* in which Thomas Wyatt's and Henry Howard, Earl of Surrey's poems, among others, are thankfully preserved.

Also, poor Yorick

Yorick's heart is moved: how beautiful, he says,
And grasps then what it must mean to be human
Returning rested from the afterlife
Into the lovely dew of resurrection.
Bare feet, with the worms and roots still in them,
The puddles cool between their metatarsals.

The skulls bay with joy, and all are grinning,
Popping their knuckles, counting their vertebrae,
And now they dance alone and now join hands,
And as they dance there, in their ribs and rigging
In each grey skeleton a robin perches
Plumping its feathers, pulsing out its song

Red, and the twittering's blood as well as music.
– Never has he witnessed a scene so vital,
The dance of life the scripture guaranteed.
Faster as shadows shorten and noon rises
The skeletons spin and conga into the air
Making a cloud, a halo on the sun.

He takes his spade and sets it on his shoulder.
He's old. Till now he's known so much regret.
He's buried his grandparents and his parents,
His kings and queens, his brothers and his friends,
His lovers, all of them, consumables,
Cinis pulvis nihil, the bones bearing

In their chalk wholeness so much love and light.
In his own graveyard, with the dear departed
One unfamiliar skeleton stands up
Tall, gracious, folding down his finger bones
Over two holes; where his hurt feet strike stone,
Sparks from the rusty nails, and in his side

A spear, perch for a phoenix. Jesus Christ
Risen in this garden, and the wounds,
Or the bones that keep the marks of wounds, are singing.
It's noon, there are no shadows. This is true.
He raised them and himself is rising up.
Also, poor Yorick. That was judgement, it is over.

Later in the day the Prince arrives,
Stepping from his script as from a carriage
Drawn up among the holes in which the dead
Waited, and from which they are all delivered,
Just like an audience when the play is over
Elbowing their coats into the dark.

Anxious, a bit deranged, he finds occasion
To hold a conversation with a skull.
Is it a skull or a stone that looks like a skull?
The heads are all gone to heaven, Jesus too,
The sexton himself put off his flesh and followed.
(Ophelia was already on her star.)

Poor prince, alone with just a book of ballads,
With just the plot nothing can raise him from.

THE WRITER AND THE TEACHER

Hanif Kureishi

f it is true, as I have read somewhere, that at any one time at least two percent of the population are writing novels, then many questions about 'creative writing' courses, and their recent rapid proliferation are really about what you need other people for.

Is writing something you do alone, or do you need others to help? You can have both useful and repetitive conversations with yourself, and you can have sex with yourself, though it might cause alarm if you claimed to be making love to yourself. Conversation and sex are generally thought to be more productive and unpredictable with others. Several of the most significant art forms of the twentieth century – jazz, pop, cinema – have been collaborative. Is writing like this or is it something else altogether?

Some people become writers because they want to be independent; they want neither to be competitive nor to rely on others. For them writing is an entirely personal self-exploration, a way of being alone, of thinking through their life, and perhaps of hiding, while speaking to someone in their head. And certainly, without a passion for solitude no writer is going to be able to bear the tedious obsessionality of his profession.

Yet that's not where the story ends, in solitude. Particularly when they are first beginning to write, some students like to show their work to their friends, and, sometimes, to their family, both as a way of informing them of certain truths, but also in the hope of a helpful reaction. Yet, however much the well-meaning reader might like the work, it doesn't follow that he will have the vocabulary to be able to speak usefully about it, saying something which might help the writer move forwards. Kindness may be comforting, but it isn't always inspiring.

Men and women have always searched for ways to enhance, modify or transform their states of mind, using herbs, nicotine, alcohol and drugs, as well as bolts of electricity through the skull, opium, baths, tonics, books and conversation. Even 'pearl cordial' – powdered pearl – was popular in the eighteenth century, as a purported cure for depression. There's no reason why the practise of writing can't help people see what's inside them, as well as helping them organise and deepen their ideas of who they are. Reading does this too, providing a vocabulary of ideas which you might utilise to view your life in a new way. But a writing teacher is not a therapist, listening patiently for the unconscious in a free association or dream telling, and the student would be surprised to learn the teacher saw himself as a healer rather than as an instructor.

When necessary, and it is usually necessary, the teacher has to teach, to pass over information about structure, voice, point of view, contrast, character, or the discipline of writing. But, particularly on those occasions when faced with a mass of work she can't understand, and doesn't know how to begin addressing – particularly horrifying for a teacher who might be under the misapprehension that she must understand, and quickly too - she might use something like a Socratic method. By asking numerous questions, the teacher will give the student her work back in a different form, making it seem both clearer and more puzzling.

Students are often at a loss when you ask them what a particular image or piece of dialogue means, and whether it is doing what they believe it is doing. While it might be productive to write from the unconscious where the world is weirder and less constrained, the work has also to be assessed rationally. Discussing it is part of this.

In a short film he'd made, a film student had stationed two young men on a park bench where he filmed them from behind – the backs of their heads – for some time. When I asked him why the shot was so sustained, he replied that the moment – to me a considerable moment – represented 'death'. He said he wanted the viewer, at this point in the film, to consider their own death. Always up for that, but trying to remain calm, and reminding myself of the nobility of teaching, I said it defeated me how he thought an audience would leap from the picture he presented to this thought. He seemed to see he needed more vivid and accurate images to convey what he wanted to say. It was also helpful for him to be told that he needed to develop a sense of story, rather than slamming scenes together in the hope the audience might notice some connection. If nothing else quite succeeds in a piece of work – humour, for instance, or the fascination of the characters – the story alone might still hold the reader's interest, as it does with soap-operas.

HANIF KUREISHI

This student might have also benefited from better authorities, from closer contact with other artists and dead poets, from whom he might learn more imaginative solutions as he strove to carry his internal world into the outside one. It is amazing that students are so rarely taught to see the connection between studying others and their own work. Borrowing a voice, or trying out new ones, isn't the same as acquiring your own, but it's a step in that direction. What you steal becomes yours when it is creatively modified. Since almost anything can usefully feed an artist, a broad humanistic education, a sort of foundation course involving religion, psychology and literature, would be a positive accompaniment to any writing course.

Conversations with a teacher should enable the student to get an idea of what an ordinary reader might make of her work, and how she must bear in mind that, in the end, she is writing for others. Writers are entertainers rather than exhibitionists. These exchanges should also give the student an idea of what she is striving to say.

The clarity a student might gain, along with new ideas, can also be obtained from writers working in groups. While concentrated individual teaching is usually preferable – most advice about writing is too general and is along the lines of 'write about what you know' – the advantage of the group is that each student has the opportunity to hear a range of criticism and suggestion, some of it mad, some invaluable. The students learn from one another.

Another version of this is for the students to work in pairs, reading their work to one another, though this is not easy with longer pieces, and difficult to keep going over the considerable period it might take to complete a sizeable work. What must be recognised is that the reader orients the writer, and the writer should understand he exists only in relation to the one whose attention is being solicited. The reader or spectator must be convinced by the competence of the writer, acknowledging that his work is credible, and that it's safe to believe it. What the writer wants is for the reader to feel as he felt.

When attempting to write there are some mistakes you have to make, mistakes which will yield good ideas, opening up a space for more thoughts. And there are other mistakes it might be worth avoiding, though sometimes it is difficult to tell the two apart. What might make it clear is when the writer gets blocked or stuck. A student of mine wanted to tell a story in the voice of a seven-year old. As you can imagine, she was finding this inordinately difficult, and it was holding up her progress. That which you most urgently want to say might not make the best writing. By trying to inhabit a point of view it was almost impossible for her to see from, she was getting little work done and becoming discouraged. Good advice would have been for her either to see if she could get hold of the the story from another position, or work on something else for a time, before returning to the idea.

She might then have to learn how to wait for the occurrence of a better idea. And this question of waiting, for a writer, is an important one. A good idea might suggest itself suddenly, but its working out or testing, will take the time it needs. It might appear to acquaintances of the author that he's doing little but lying on the sofa staring into the distance, or going on long walks. Clearly, Charles Dickens was writing when he was walking. This might be when good ideas turn up – a book is a thousand inspirations rather than one big one - and the guilt of fertile indolence has to be borne.

Writing and life are not separate, though they can be separated, and, on the whole, it is the teacher's job to consider the writing as an independent entity. Often though, a student will use writing to think about his life, so that what the student is showing the teacher is a problem.

A woman decides to write about her mother but finds herself overwhelmed with grief and heartache. She pushes on, but stops, terrified of what she might want to say. Eventually she must decide whether or not to drop this painful but essential subject. Perhaps she'd prefer to write something else. Or she might need to discover whether she can endure the difficulty of confronting the matter. And it might also occur to her: is writing a way of calming terror, or of creating it? We can see here that the writer is the material; the poem is the person. They are the same thing.

Following on from this, an anxiety in the writer will be a fear of what his words will do to others, and what others might do to him in return if he says what he thinks, even in fictional form. As there are certain ideas which are discouraged or forbidden in families, and indeed in all institutions, most adults – even if only unconsciously – are afraid of expressing their own ideas about what is going on. They fear they will be accused of betrayal and then punished - both of which are possible. They will have to wonder whether they are prepared to put up with this. A certain personal truth might, however, be what the writer most wants to reveal, thus creating an intolerable conflict which might lead to a block.

If a student can only write miserable monologues at the end of which the speaker kills himself, you might wonder, not only about the student's state of mind, but also about why there aren't any other characters in the piece, about the voices which aren't being heard. Obviously this student – who had been through the psychiatric system where he wasn't much listened to – was showing me something I had to take seriously and think hard about. It was worrying, and not easy for me to see how to proceed here.

Eventually I persuaded the student to bring in other characters to make more of a conversation of it. To his credit, after a few weeks, he was able to do this, though the suicides continued. I learned that when the unsayable was about to be broached at last, suicide was seen as the convenient way out. It was like a version of writer's block. But once his characters began to have exchanges – and the student saw the point of debating with himself, of opening up his own head – his work developed. The scenes got longer and the people spoke. His work became more available to others.

For a while at least, a measure of madness appeared to have been transferred from the writer to his characters. They were iller than he was. Certainly it's not the most healthy who are the most creative. As Proust reminded us, 'Everything great in the world comes from neurotics. We enjoy a thousand intellectual delicacies, but we have no idea of their cost, to those who invented them, in sleepless nights, tears, spasmodic laughter, rashes, asthmas, epilepsies, and the fear of death, which is worse than all the rest.'

It was my student's excitement and determination in his work which reassured me. Our meetings were a helpful structure. I think without a teacher to accompany him through this, he could have twisted in painful circles and become more isolated. As it was, his work was among the most imaginative and strange I've read, far removed from the dull realism and conventionality which most students think passes for imaginative work.

Some students have considerable phantasies about becoming a writer, of what they think being a writer will do for them. This quickens their desire, and helps them to get started. But when the student begins to get an idea of how difficult it is to complete a considerable piece of work – to write fifteen thousand good words, while becoming aware of the more or less impossibility of making significant money from writing – she will experience a dip, or 'crash' and become discouraged and feel helpless. The loss of a phantasy can be painful, but if the student can get through it – if the teacher can show the student that there's something good in her work and help her endure the frustration of learning to do something difficult – the student will make better progress.

In the end, the writer mostly teaches himself and will always want to develop, finding new forms for his interests. If he's lucky, along with learning to allow his imagination free reign, he'll mostly edit and evaluate his own work himself. Of course it doesn't follow that he'll never need anyone else. He might prefer to ignore others, but he will need to listen to them first, as he continues to speak.

POETRY

DAVID SERGEANT

A Breach

A breach, everywhere occurring, for someone
The sky ripped open, as was expected
And impossible. You will know what I mean.
Come back when you hear them say *dead*.

They want me to be humble, down to earth,
To write about the egg upon his beard.
But I see filmic rips, the day like breath
Rehealing over steamed-up glass that's nudged

But not before you've glimpsed a space beyond
And readjusted. Bright face who's gone,
This is natural as grass and wonderful
As roses. The world shakes like a heart
With every door-slam, exiting or start,
I touch it trembling until I follow.

BOOK WORLD

THE ITALIAN JOB

Thomas Corcoran

One of the most striking differences between Italian and English high street culture lies in the number of small bookshops that you will find in any major Italian city. Turin is no exception, and, indeed, on my own little street we have a pretty decent little bookshop a few doors down – though I must shamefully admit I have only actually gone in there to attempt (and fail) to use the photocopier.

This tendency towards the proliferation of bookshops is particularly evident on the large *via Po*, near the university area, where you will find bookshop after bookshop and you will also find book streetstalls lining the *portici*, where you may haggle with a series of extremely grumpy old merchants (over for example, the appropriate level of price reduction for a 1978 edition of Italo Calvino's *La giornata di uno scrutator* when it is missing the middle seventeen pages.) Even in the little Piedmonte town of Pinerolo, which has 30,000 inhabitants, I saw no less than 5 privately-owned bookshops on my *giro* of the town. Indeed, bookshops are not just in the usual places, but come in interesting shapes and sizes. You will often find a bookshop in train stations and metro stations, and even in public underground toilet corridors – proving that the Italian desire for books is diminished not even by the imminent threat of bumping into a man in the act of defacation and/or self-prostitution. Now that is some serious *dedizione*.

Furthermore, in an area of particular interest to a dyed-in-the-wool classicist such as yours truly, I am most impressed by the quality of the average bookshop's classics collection, and, indeed, by the average Italian bookshop-worker's knowledge of classical literature. It's very different in Britain, where my request to be shown the 'Classics collection' will usually result in either a) an enthusiastic but entirely misplaced direction towards such classics as *The Complete Works of G.K. Chesterton*, or b) a look of hatred/fear/anger, as if to say 'You're not related to Boris Johnson, are you?' and 'I bet you have an alarming level of interest in adolescent boys'. This doesn't really substitute for what I get in Italy: an individual expressing genuine interest in classical literature, who will have read a decent selection themselves, and who will be able to discuss the advantages and disadvantages of the various editions. Let Mayor Johnson teach Latin to knife-criminals – but this is all I really ask for from a society.

Of course, I am a gentleman of very lowly means, and so I usually have to resort to either that most English way of using a bookshop – looking without buying – or, alternatively, that most Italian way – shoplifting. However, it's very easy to get your hands on a book at reduced prices. In the corridors of *Palazzo Nuovo* (the famously-hideous main teaching building of the *Università di Torino*), I managed to get my hands on some Italian books for a mere 6.90 euros, which, minus the sensational collapse of the pound sterling, would normally be about £5. I bought a copy of P. A. Brunt's *La Caduta della Repubblica romana* (*The Fall of the Roman Republic*), largely because I had already read it in English and felt that it thus might make a good first academic book to read in Italian. As it happened, it didn't, because I soon remembered that Brunt (like many an Italian academic) is in the end a bit of a stuffy old Marxist. This was probably the reason the book was on sale in the first place, given that next to it was a stall run by a Communist youth league, whose members were attempting to flog me various books by some rather tedious German-Jewish classicist called Karl something-or-other. I bought *Il Secolo delle Donne* (*The Century of Women*), of a feminist-minded work, which gained me a degree of kudos with the Leftists – though I have to admit my main motivation in buying it was because I quite liked the pictures of pretty Italians ladies learning to ride bicycles.

To the detriment of the British proletariat and their hopes of revolution, Communist youth leagues are not a very common occurrence in a British university foyer. But the following two facts are to the unjustifiable detriment of every single one of us members of the self-repressed tea-drinking races who have ever been in a university – firstly, that books are probably even more scarce than Communists in a university foyer, and secondly, that local bookshops in British cities are scarcer than either. I can honestly say that in four years studying at Oxford, I never once walked through a corridor in a university building and came across somebody trying to sell me a book. Maybe I just don't look like the right sort of customer, but given that I'm the kind of guy who tucks his jumper into his trousers, I think that this is not a very likely explanation. Indeed I can remember coming across very few local bookshops at all in Oxford, other than an admittedly-excellent Blackwells (a local bookshop, on the technicality that it is the first ever Blackwells store). In the other British university town I have lived in, St. Andrews, it is exactly the same story: perhaps one or two dingy places run by a left-over aristocratic hippy or Serbian war criminal in hiding, and that's it. And take a look at Liverpool, which is, in many ways, the English equivalent of Turin (in the industrial North of the country, combining large internal migrant populations with large external ones, and the proud possesser of a football team with a penchant for winning the European Cup) and yet has barely a fraction of the number of bookshops.

I suppose that I should end my (truly British) anti-patriotic attack on my own nation, and try to be more constructive. Why do Italian bookshops thrive? Well, there are some very clear smaller reasons – not least the appalling state of the postal service, which means that internet providers like Amazon haven't really caught on. But really, you've got to look at the bigger socio–economic differences between Italy and England. In short, big business simply isn't so big here. Oh, for sure, a heck of a lot of the country is owned by that world-reknowned comedic billionaire and *presidente del consiglio*, Silvio Berlusconi, but beyond this, there is still a very strong small-business and – shun not the phrase – artisanal class. Whereas only about 2% of the British workforce works in a firm with 12 or less employees, in Italy it's more like 20%, and thus a large chunk of the population is still involved in producing and selling their goods locally.

Needless to say, this economic difference affects the society and culture at large. You cannot buy fresh bread or any decent fruit in a supermarket – you have to go to a local bread shop or the local market, which run daily in nearly all urban residential areas, rich and poor. There are no real equivalents to Boots, Debenhams or Tesco, and a (non-Italian) friend of mine recounted to me a telling story from his time at La Sapienza university in Rome. An (also non-Italian) professor displayed a chart measuring the level of globalisation in various countries through a comparison of their number of Starbucks stores. After 5 minutes, a number of the Italian students put their hands up, and one asked, 'What's Starbucks?' The academic had so clearly assumed that Starbucks had penetrated all of the Western World that he didn't even bother to check if it had set up stores in the country in which he was lecturing! Italians, in stark contrast to the Britons (who may go weeks at a time without spending a single shekel outside a big business) simply prefer goods that are produced on a small scale, even if it they are more expensive.

And so, in such an economy and society, little bookshops can survive. While there are great big Italian *catena* bookshops, like the superb Feltrinelli stores, they will never be able to compete with the little bookshops on the latter's unique selling-point: precisely that they ARE little bookshops! Italians buy books because they like books, not because they want to fill up a bourgeois bookcase. Many Italians tend to view books less academically than their British counterparts, as something that forms a crucial part part of everybody's lifestyle culture. Thus in Italian, you don't refer to a good book as a *buon libro* (good book) but as a *bel libro* (beautiful book). In this way, I don't think that Italians would ever go in for the new Anglo-fad of buying digital books, as they would probably dislike the loss of pleasure of actually owning the aesthetically-pleasing object that is a well-constructed book. Italy gives you the feeling of a culture where books are wanted and needed – not the feigned reserve of a cultural elite, but something for the use and abuse of everyone as he or she should see fit. Just as Italians will regularly ask you, with an entirely genuine tone of inquistiveness, why anybody would ever want to buy a meal at MacDonalds, they simply don't understand why anybody would cut themselves off from the reading culture – it would be like giving up espresso!

Italy is very far from perfect. The often-irrational status quo that has held sway in the country for the past twenty years, finding its apex in Berlusconi-ism (that strange mixture of cultural-conservatism, socialistic economics, anarchic corruption, post-*Fascismo*, and personality cult) has left Italy with huge problems, not least the national debt of (literally) 116%, the Mafia-driven scandals, and the disgraceful ongoing popularity of 1980s pop music. But there have been good things among the bad. I think that when we look back on Berlusconi-ist Italy in the future, we may remember parts of it more fondly than the current sex scandals and rubbish-lined streets of Napoli would suggest – as a place which ultimately held out as a bastion for our European culture against the march of globalisation, retaining the kind of wealth that cannot be measured on the scales of the *Economist Magazine*, but which is all the more precious for that. I would posit the preservation of the bookshop culture as one such crucial achievement. For some, that's a small victory, but for me, it's one of the fundamental things that ensure Italy remains not just some other country, but one of the greatests nations in the world. So, here's a salute to *il fiore del artigiano*, a cry of *forza libri*! and a big, boisterous expression of *complimenti* to the bookshop-dotted nation of *Italia*.

ALISON
BRACKENBURY

POETRY

ALISON BRACKENBURY

A bad patch

How hopeful to look back. Hope for the white-clad baby
So blonde, quick-witted, maybe
Future would steer their days
As the great liners blaze.

The baby's hair grew dark,
Her hands began to shake.
Life ran aground in narrow
North-facing bungalows.

With tall trees, dust-bathed hens,
How they were happy then.
The swing twirled on its rope.
Hope is its end, I hope.

THE OLD POEM

ROBERT BURNS, 'JOHN ANDERSON MY JO'

I

John Anderson my jo, John,
   When we were first acquaint,
Your locks were like the raven,
   Your bonnie brow was brent;   [*brent*, smooth]
But now your brow is beld, John,
   Your locks are like the snaw,
But blessings on your frosty pow,   [*pow*, head]
   John Anderson my jo!

II

John Anderson my jo, John,
   We clamb the hill thegither,
And monie a cantie day, John,   [*cantie*, happy]
   We've had wi' ane anither;
Now we maun totter down, John,
   And hand in hand we'll go,
And sleep thegither at the foot,
   John Anderson my jo!

T o make the choice of 'old poem' less arbitrary, I have recently observed centenaries but in doing so neglected
the half-hundreds and so overlooked the birth of Burns
in 1759, for which, I apologise to all lovers of poetry as
well as Scots. This song is based on a traditional verse
of which there exists an obscene version (in the *Oxford Book of Scottish
Poetry*) as also a political travesty attributed to Burns himself. But here
it becomes an unusual celebration of sustained married love, a mutual
devotion 'for better or worse, for richer for poorer, in sickness and in
health', as the old wedding service put it. It is written in the Scottish
tongue so many readers have to get used to some unfamiliar words but
the 'little language' is essential to the warmth and intimacy of the lines,
like the poetry of William Barnes or the love talk of Mellors in *Lady
Chatterley*. Memory retains the speaker's pride in her husband's youth-
ful glamour in stanza one and the happiness they earlier shared in two.
But though the present in the second half of each verse shows the 'now'
as loss, the deprivation forces out a love that seems the deeper by its
resistance. 'Blessings on your frosty pow' strengthens the apparently
conventional image of locks like snow. Horror at the cold, at the end
of the so-called 'little Ice Age', recurs in Burns's poetry. Those repeated
'buts' dramatise the change just as in verse two the 'ands' offer an in-
crement to offset what is taken away. To climb is usually thought harder
work than the descent of a hill yet physical strength made the ascent a
pleasure whereas now they must 'totter down'. The slight comedy of the
image though adds to the wonderful image of the penultimate line, that
they will 'sleep thegither at the foot'. 'O death where is thy sting' when
they end in sleeping together like any young groom and bride. Maybe
to comment on so open a poem is as otiose as explaining a joke but my
excuse is that this is not the folk tradition itself but Burns's tribute to it,
tightening the sinews he recognises in it.

Read more Burns of course, especially in the Canongate Classics
edition, not simply the songs but the tale 'Tom o' Shanter' and the verse
epistles, that very literary genre, which he uses to honour the makers
of performance poetry as we would now call it with the same depth
of response and thought to be found in 'To a Mouse' or 'To a Louse'.
For satire, which observes the close relation of religious enthusiasm to
sexual excitement read 'The Holy Fair' or 'Holy Willie's Prayer' and for
revolutionary fire 'A Man's a Man for a' that' and 'The Twa Dogs'.

REVIEWS

SURVIVAL OF THE BOOK

The Oxford Companion to English Literature, ed. Dinah Birch
OUP, 2009
ISBN 978-0192806871

Brian Nellist

Like the other Good Book, *The Oxford Companion to English Literature* has gone through many versions, this is the seventh, yet continues to bear some of the finger prints of the original deviser, Sir Paul Harvey, not least the synopses, if now abbreviated, of all Scott's novels. Everyone interested in literature probably has at least one of the previous editions and I'm comparing this one with my battered copy of the fifth. Almost all reference books have pages one never uses but the new edition has no dead areas. Gone are the essays on censorship, now of only historical interest, and those baffling tables to determine the dates of Easter in a particular year. In their place is a welcome chronology of principal works alongside major events starting from the year 1000. The reader is ushered in with a series of stimulating and wide-ranging essays on current trends, on post-colonial and children's writing, which can mention authors not named in the main text.

If literature exists between the particularities of history and the ideas of philosophy then the *Companion* has always been more of a history of English literature, but the national adjective has always been generously interpreted and the new volume is more inclusive than ever of overseas writing. Most people interested in serious literature in their own tongue are concerned also with literature in general. Homer, Dante and Tolstoy become part of our common experience. Galdós and Machado were missing from my old Fifth and of course, I also wanted

Machado de Assis; much always wants more, as I used to be warned. What is new also is the wider reference to what purists loftily used to dismiss as 'Popular Culture', a much fuller inclusiveness of SF and of children's writers (including Enid Blyton; don't frown so, Sir Paul). Selection has been made partly on the basis of categories and genres, the great expansion of travel writing, for instance, so inevitably some good writing that escapes such definition is absent, Oliver Sacks and Simon Schama. But it is all too easy in any such volume to spot gaps created by one's own tastes and interests. Instead be thankful for the greatly expanded series of entries on musical settings of English poems (Hullo! here's Finzi at last) and for the really helpful characterisation of the work of contemporary poets. By consulting the index you can find, generally, who wrote or revised the entries. All right, Mary Daryush (who?) and W. W. Jacobs have dropped out but space has to be made for new entrants and a certain Darwinian severity becomes necessary. Film and theatrical groups, the Théâtre de Complicité for example, are an appropriate exchange. The entry for every author of scale includes a brief reference to recent scholarship. Sharp eyes have made the volume surprisingly up-to-the-minute. Publication was in time to include Hilary Mantel's *Wolf Hall* though not so advanced in 2009 to record it as a Booker prize-winner in the welcome concluding lists.

Some will argue that the Internet supplies the information they need but here the ascription of articles to authors guarantees reliability. Even more importantly there is nothing attractive about a computer screen whereas this is a beautiful piece of book production, with generous margins and spaces between the entries, very different from my old cramped fifth edition. It celebrates not only the survival of the book itself but also the pleasure a book can give as well as the ease with which the information you seek can be retrieved. Of course, keep also your old version of the work, if you already have one, because they are different books and you may just want to find what date Easter fell on in 1565. But you must have the new one as well and certainly give it as a present to anyone intending to read English at university, to friends and relations in reading groups, or even someone who has remained sceptical of the importance of literature. The breadth and detail and interest of this book will make converts.

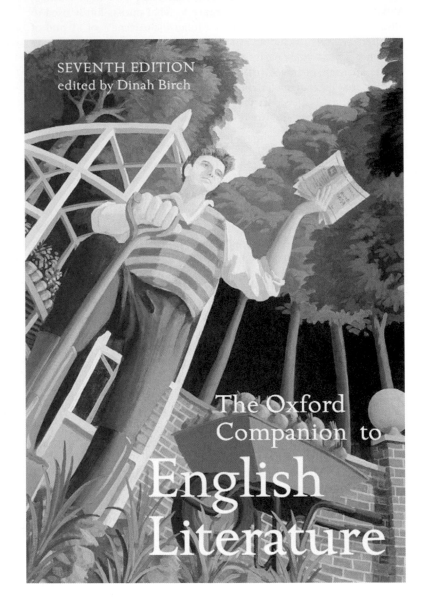

SEVENTH EDITION
edited by Dinah Birch

The Oxford
Companion to
English
Literature

REVIEWS

KEEPING COMPANY
WITH THE OXFORD COMPANION TO ENGLISH LITERATURE

Katy Hooper

Back in 2005, offered the task of being Dinah Birch's editorial assistant as she took on the editorship of *The Oxford Companion to English Literature*, I estimated that it would take an afternoon a week – easy to fit in with a part-time job at the University Library and children at school. By the time the seventh edition was published in September 2009, the *Companion* had become a daily, and frequently nightly presence, following us as we moved house, and went on holiday, and trying the patience of teenagers regaled with 'curious *Companion* fact of the day'.

In many ways, my role was to keep track of the enterprise by turning words into numbers. The huge volume of entries from the previous edition to be revisited, revised and perhaps rejected, from *'Aaron's Rod'* to 'Zwingli, Ulrich', became a spreadsheet of numbered headwords into which new entries could be added. That way, spellings could be modernised ('a High – not 'hye' – Way to the Spital House') and names changed to more current forms (Zélide now appears under 'Charrière, Isabelle de') without the risk of duplicating, or, worse, losing an entry between editions. The seventh edition now stands at more than 7,000 entries, from Abbey Theatre, Dublin to Zweig, Stefan, and over 1,000 of those are new.

Counting the words was vital, too; those new entries accounted for about 10% of the volume's total of well over one million words, which had to be shared appropriately between the different areas of editorial responsibility, and within them. Colourful pie charts showed which area took the largest slice – not surprisingly the Victorian entries – but the eighteenth century followed close behind, with many of the longest entries devoted to the individual speeches of politicians. Space had to be found for new entries in every area, and especially in the growth areas of travel writing, biography, science fiction and fantasy, children's literature and black British and postcolonial literature. Cutting the wordcount wherever possible was essential, which often meant that a headword in the spreadsheet now represented an entirely rewritten article. 'De-tweeding' was the eighteenth century editor's apt description of this refocusing and updating of the retained entries.

The five years between beginning and end of the task coincided with our discovery of a charity which rescues historic buildings, landmarks in their area, and restores them just enough to give them a new purpose as short-term holiday lets, without compromising their uniqueness or character. Finding ways to let people live for a few days in a Jacobean tower, a pineapple-shaped eighteenth-century folly, or a medieval hall – to inhabit these astonishing survivals of their time – seemed to me a similar task to the reshaping of the *Companion*. The texts it surveys have also survived over centuries, were landmarks in their contemporary landscapes (*Jessica's First Prayer* (1866) sold two million copies in the author's lifetime) and are still worth discovering, getting inside, can give their readers a new perspective.

As a reader, working on the *Companion* has introduced me to an eclectic selection of books that did not feature on my undergraduate literature course, but which I am now determined to track down, intrigued by their author's entries – Bernard Mandeville's *Enquiry into the Origin of Honour* (1732) or Penelope Fitzgerald's *The Bookshop* (1978), for example. I am also more aware of the authors I've never read, so, browsing through the local library's sale of old stock, I'm happy to find Stanley Middleton's *Changes and Chances*, Helen Dunmore's *The Siege*, Buchi Emecheta's *The Joys of Motherhood* and *Confessions of Zeno* by Italo Svevo – a small tower to add to the reading pile for future holidays.

THE READING REVOLUTION

DIARIES OF THE READER ORGANISATION

Eleanor Stanton

I am a fairly new member of staff at The Reader Organisation; still learning the ropes. I'm working from Toxteth Library – for Liverpool Libraries and TRO – to develop GIR groups in that community. Over the past weeks I have visited many different read-aloud groups, immersing myself in the Get Into Reading (GIR) spirit – from open-to-anyone sessions in libraries to targeted groups in specific settings; from poetry and songs with dementia sufferers to reading short stories aloud in a drug detox centre.

Now I have started to set up my own groups – I facilitate a group in a mental health in-patient service, which is attended by both staff and service users. Recently we read a short story called 'The Door' by Helen Simpson, in which a recently bereaved woman finds comfort and kindness in a man who comes to replace her back door. We talk about who we open up to and why. Someone comments that it is often easier to reveal things to strangers than to those we know well. 'The Door' wasn't a universal hit. One man, halfway through the reading, was adamant: 'No. It's not for me. I don't like it.' But at the end he preferred – a tad grudgingly but still with changed mind – 'It got better as more was revealed'. I wondered whether he would have persevered if he had been reading alone. Sometimes someone else's energy is necessary to get you through to the thing you most need. 'I enjoyed that,' he said of the group's discussion. 'It's good to do something stimulating rather than just watching the TV.'

This is something I'm finding out both from inside and outside. Recently, I attended a Read to Lead workshop in Cardiff. Being read to alongside ten other adults is probably an alien concept for most people, and until lately, it was for me too. More than a few remarked that the last time they were read to was as a child, yet for all that strangeness, something happened in that room. The words, read aloud and discussed between us, took on a beauty and resonance I think I would have missed had I been reading alone. Later we were asked to share a poem or short piece of prose with the group. For me it was 'The Call' by Charlotte Mew, a poem that I had been struck by when a colleague read it out in one of their GIR groups, and I have read it again many times since. In that group, some had found the poem to be about death, some about the break-up of a relationship. Perhaps I agreed with them at the time, but now as I sat reading it to my fellow workshop attendees,I felt for the first time a totally different message – one of release and freedom, especially in these central lines of the poem:

> **To-night we heard a call,**
> **A rattle on the window-pane,**
> **A voice on the sharp air,**
> **And felt a breath stirring our hair,**
> **A flame within us: Something swift and tall**
> **Swept in and out and that was all.**
> **Was it a bright or a dark angel? Who can know?**
> **It left no mark upon the snow,**
> **But suddenly it snapped the chain**
> **Unbarred, flung wide the door**
> **Which will not shut again;**
> **And so we cannot sit here any more.**
> **We must arise and go.**

It's these lines that are stirring: 'Suddenly it... flung wide the door / Which will not shut again'. The feeling of awe or fear is right, it seems to me, no matter whether the experience comes from a bright or dark source. After all, the poem is talking about a moment of change that cannot be undone. When she says it 'will not shut again', it means she must have tried to close the door, but the choice to remain with the status quo has been taken away. Although this may be frightening, it also liberating. For me, the 'breath stirring our hair', which seems such a little and inconsequential thing, makes the impact of the unbarring and flinging of the door all the greater. On the page, the poem has a kind of strength. Read aloud with others, the newness and the command seem imperative. I have always been a (silent) reader of books but I recognise the power of sharing literature in this new and unfamiliar way. What must it be like for those who have not been readers at all?

I am currently engaged with meeting people who live or work in my catchment area to try and get reading groups up and running in the library. Very soon, these groups will be launched. I need to choose, for the first sessions, materials that will at once grab and enthuse the readers. I think, for one such session, I will read the short story, *Penny in the Dust* by Ernest Buckler and then Robert Hayden's *Those Winter Sundays*.

THE READING REVOLUTION

POETRY: A PLACE OF REFUGE

Patrick Scott-Graham

Professors, doctors, teachers, people with few formal qualifications, those who have never attended school, with different beliefs and of varying ages, walk through the doors of Asylum Link, a Liverpool-based charity drop-in centre each week. Everyone has a different story and different reasons why they have come to Liverpool. How can a group of people from all corners of the globe, sitting in a room in rainy Liverpool, overcome their language and cultural divisions? Asylum seekers come to the UK from many different countries – Rwanda, Afghanistan, Iraq, Iran, Sudan, Zimbabwe, and Eritrea to name a few. Not only do these countries have different values, languages and dialects but individual asylum seekers are *people*, individuals who come from diverse family, social and cultural backgrounds.

As part of my final year English dissertation project, which involved facilitating a Get into Reading (GIR) group with some of Asylum Link's visitors, I found poetry to be a strong way to reach for common, human ground between people. In our weekly reading sessions, we began by reading through a chosen poem a number of times. People would take turns reading the text aloud individually and we would also read the text together. We would talk over words we did not understand and discuss their meanings. By the end of the project, we were using a dictionary to help find definitions – a shared object, which anyone could reach for, at any time. When people became confident with the language in the text, we went onto discuss our favourite lines and the reasons for our choices.

My involvement with the project lasted for sixteen sessions, from October 2007 until January 2008. A core group of five people attended regularly: an Afghan man (A), an Iranian couple with only basic English (H, I), a Rwandan woman (F) and a Zimbabwean woman (Q). They joined for various reasons: because they had loved literature back home; because they wanted to find out more about English literature; because they wanted to read texts from different cultures in translation. They were dedicated to the reading task and became confident together and keen to participate in discussions.

One memorable session took place before Christmas. A, F, H and Q were present. We looked at Wendy Cope's '30th December':

**At first I'm startled by the sound of bicycles
Above my head. And then I see them, two swans
Flying in to their runway behind the reeds.**

**The bridge is slippery, the grass so sodden
That water seeps into my shoes. But now
The sun has come out and everything is calm
And beautiful as the end of a hangover.**

**Christmas was a muddle
Of turkey bones and muted quarrelling.**

**The visitors have left.
Solitary walkers smile and tell each other
That the day is wonderful.**

**If only this could be Christmas now –
These shining meadows,
The hum of huge wings in the sky.**

I asked the group what they thought the most important sections of the poem were. A said that *hangover* related to 'nature reflecting on you, as the changes in your life take place'. Q also saw the great importance of *hangover*. She suggested the poem was about asylum. She explained that many problems are described, but then the hangover comes. Christmas then becomes related to the idea of visitors and focuses on changes in people. She said asylum problems could be forgotten, at least temporarily, as a result of this respect for change. She explained that Christmas is a time when all humans come together, including 'Born Agains, non-Born Agains – everyone'. F agreed and explained this was similar in Rwanda – people of all faiths come together to celebrate Christmas.

We went on to talk about cultural festivals in other countries. A described the Spring Festival in Afghanistan, while H talked about Iran's Winter Feast, both happy occasions. A, a Muslim, took a particular interest in F and Q as they talked about Rwandan and Zimbabwean Christmas celebrations, which involve going to church and eating well.

H said most of the poem held a lot of happiness for him. He liked the two swans and the sun coming out but he found the third stanza difficult and uncomfortable to read. This was because of the word *bones*, which, he said, relates to death. At the session's end, H said the poem was 'like waves'. 'It is like reality,' he said, gesturing an up and down movement with his hand.

In other sessions, we looked at Byron's 'The Wild, the Free'; Frost's 'The Road Not Taken'; a section from Omar Khayyam's 'Rubaiyat' and Shaaban Robert's 'Swahili', both in translation. By the end of the project in January, I noticed changes in the core participants' confidence. A, who had been reserved, was making friends with other participants. H and I had gone from shy to outgoing and confident with their English. Some of the participants said the sessions had made them happy. That seemed an achievement.

The Asylum Link project has carried on throughout 2008, with a new facilitator and new funding. It will allow asylum seekers to continue reaching for human ideas and emotions through literature. I found it one of the best things I have done and the work really enhanced my experience as a student of literature. Highly recommended.

MAKE FRIENDS WITH A BOOK

Janet Westcott

I t started with Blake Morrison's article in *The Guardian*[1] – how wonderful, I thought, that's what I want to do. So I went to Jane Davis's course in Oxford and leapt from there. I'm part of the Poole Libraries' Development Team (a grand name for 4-and-a-bit librarians!). We are responsible for developing the service in line with the Borough of Poole's priorities, and Get into Reading (GIR) particularly helps us with reducing social isolation, promoting well-being, and extending library services to older people.

I had previously met with Poole's Gateway team who provide services for people with mild and moderate mental illness. They had picked up from local GPs that there was a significant number of older people in Broadstone who were presenting at the surgeries with symptoms including anxiety and depression, linked to their isolation. As the library in Broadstone is right next to the two GP surgeries, (and our biggest branch) this seemed the ideal location to pilot our first GIR group. And so **Make Friends with a Book** was born.

I contacted the practice managers of both surgeries, who were very supportive. I cribbed mercilessly from the GIR website for the information I gave them, and they passed it on to the GPs and displayed posters in the surgeries. I wrote to local residential homes and sheltered housing complexes with information for the wardens and posters for the common rooms. I contacted various people in Social Services who come into contact with older people – the Primary Intervention Care Service were particularly useful as they meet people as they come out of hospital. Dorset Blind also put some publicity in their newsletter, and of course we advertised in the library.

Make Friends with a Book is promoted as a chance to sit back and relax, listen to short stories and poems and chat about what we read together. Good conversation, good company and free tea and biscuits! (I think the free tea and biscuits are crucial, and shortbread is the current favourite.) I read aloud a short story and a poem, and we chat about what we've read. Everyone has a copy and most people have something to say, though there is no pressure to do so.

Staff at Broadstone library have been very enthusiastic and one of them has taken on the reading from time to time. Apart from that, I and another team member do the reading. We are about to start reading a novel, though it took some time to get to that point – our group seem to prefer short stories, though of course it is far more staff intensive to find a new story every week. Please readers, do send in any suggestions.

We started at the beginning of August with 5 people, and now regularly get up to 10 each week. I'm not sure whether we have really hit our target audience, though people have come for a variety of reasons. Two have said that they want to get back into reading after a period of being unable to read for various reasons. One wanted to make friends, and one was persuaded to continue coming although after the first week she thought that the others were too intellectual for her – she has been almost every week since. At least one was referred by the local branch of the Richmond Fellowship – a service for people with long term and continuing mental health problems. As the weeks have passed, friendships are being made, people are chatting before and after the meeting.

Following the success of this group, we are starting another one at another library which will be run by the staff there – they are a particularly enthusiastic group who are keen to get more people into their library. I've been approached by the carers' service to start a group for carers, and our flyer has been published in social services' staff newsletter. The concept seems to be striking a chord with lots of people, and I think the potential is enormous, given the resources to expand.

If you are wondering whether you have the resources to start a GIR group, I'd recommend just going for it – start small and see where the journey takes you. Make sure that you have at least two people who are willing to read aloud, in case of holidays or illness – you don't want to have to miss a week once you get started. Provide free drinks and biscuits. Use the GIR website to get inspiration for your publicity, and contact as many people and groups as you can think of. Most of all, enjoy sharing stories – it's a great joy to discuss what we've been reading, and probably why many of us became librarians in the first place.

1. Read Blake Morrison's article here:
http://www.guardian.co.uk/books/2008/jan/05/fiction.scienceandnature

BOOKS ABOUT

BATTLE

Angela Macmillan

I am writing this on Remembrance Day 2009, the first year with no living link to The Great War so that our attention has mostly been focused on the present-day sacrifice and loss of life in Afghanistan. It is too early for a body of literature to have emerged from that conflict but I have brought together books that tell the soldier's story. From World War Two to the war on terror, the best writing goes beyond exterior terrain and addresses itself to the impact of violence and fear, on the interior landscape of the individual mind.

Some of the books are out of print and can only be found online or in second hand bookshops. Don't be deterred: they are worth the search.

David Holbrook, *Flesh Wounds*   ISBN 978-1862273917

In the excellent *The Face of Battle*, John Keegan briefly refers to *Flesh Wounds* as an 'unfairly overlooked book, the first major novel to deal with D Day.' I had never heard of it and took myself off to the internet to track down a copy. It is the lightly fictionalised story of a young man whose university career is interrupted by the outbreak of war. His pre-war experience of the tenderness of love is the thing that ultimately saves him from the long-term psychological scarring effects of battle. It is worth reading for a feel of the atmosphere of 1930's Cambridge and for the extraordinary first-hand accounts of battle.

Tim O' Brien, *The Things They Carried*   ISBN 978-0006543947

The title piece of this sequence of short stories about the war in Vietnam is justifiably famous. 'How To Tell A True War Story' tackles the impossibility of giving truthful account of war; of separating 'what happened from what seemed to happen... there is always the surreal seemingness, which makes the story seem untrue, but which in fact represents the hard and exact truth as it seemed.' 'On the Rainy River', the story of a boy trying to decide whether to dodge the draft is outstandingly good. The cumulative effect of all the stories together is powerfully moving.

Mary Weston, *The Escape Plan*   ISBN 978-0704381544

This is a novel about the aftermath of the Korean War during which Tiger Sterling had been captured by the Chinese and subjected to what we now refer to as brain washing. On his release and return to Hawaii the military are afraid that he may be a Communist spy and accordingly he is attended by a government psychologist with whom he manages to strike up a lasting friendship. The novel takes you into unfamiliar territory and makes quietly compelling reading.

Michael Herr, *Dispatches*   ISBN 978-0330255738

When this non-fiction novel was first published in 1977 the *New York Times* said 'it is as if Dante had gone to hell with a cassette recording of Jimi Hendrix and a pocketful of pills.' Michael Herr, one-time war correspondent for *Esquire* magazine, takes the reader through a tour of duty in Vietnam giving ordinary soldiers a voice. The sheer absurdity and lawlessness of the US Military makes this book the most terrifying account of warfare I have ever read: Herr encounters a general who intends dropping a whole bunch of piranha into the rice paddies in the north: 'He was talking fish but his dreamy eyes were full of mega-death.'

Dexter Filkins, *The Forever War*   ISBN 978-0099523048

The author was correspondent for the *Los Angeles Times* in Afghanistan and the *New York Times* in Iraq. This compelling book, which concentrates for the large part on the war on terror in Iraq, does not rehearse the arguments for and against invasion and military occupation, instead Filkins simply reports on experience without explanation or moral judgement... and the experience is chaotic, complex and mostly terrifying. How to make sense of it, or see any resolution? You will find yourself having to talk about this book.

Also recommended:
Brian Turner, *Here Bullet* (ISBN 978-1852247997), poetry of the Iraq conflict.

YOUR REGULARS

MEG, MOG, MIDDLEMARCH

Jane Davis

For more than twenty-five years, while I was studying and teaching literature, my job was to read, to think about what I had read, and to talk to people about that. It's a terrible thing to admit, but I struggled to imagine why readers found it difficult to get into reading complex books, and sometimes thought it a failure of will: they didn't really want to. But here I am, wanting to reread George Eliot for the first time in seven or eight years, and finding it difficult to concentrate: hard paragraphs in *Middlemarch* shout less than the need to sort new staff contracts. I am going to have to devise some regular daily plan for attentive reading, because these days, like most other adults, I haven't got the concentration at the end of the day.

You might say, why bother? Isn't the active life as important as the contemplative? Yes, and having founded The Reader Organisation – a great experiment involving people and books – I am choosing the active during this part of my life, and enjoying it, too. All the same I am beginning to feel the need for some element of the contemplative life. It might come from meditation, or study, or prayer or perhaps even as the by-product of a very long walk, but contemplation's serious thinking, imagining and feeling also arises in the course of reading a complex novel or epic poem. This accosting kind of thought is a natural function of being human: babies and small children are concentrating in this way most of the time – building thought-models of reality.

On the mantelshelf I have two brass cauldrons, about the size of small tangerines, gently dented by three generations of play. They have a minutely serrated rim, which you only become aware of when you pick them up. Holding one now, running my finger around that rim, I re-feel the pleasure I had in those serrations when the cauldrons sat on my grandparents' mantelpiece. I also feel a sense of the mild fear I had of the legs of the things: sharp fat brass pencil points. Sniffing them, I remember their thin, high-metallic smell and I am back in the living room of my grandparents' house, where we went after school for tea and stories and toast. We often had the light off, to save electricity. In the dark, the cauldrons shone in the light thrown by the coal fire.

That kind of relation to those cauldrons is what the great human scientist George Eliot is talking about in *The Mill on The Floss*, when Tom comes home from his boarding school for the first time, and enjoys the vivid return of things that have always been there:

> **The happiness of seeing the bright light in the parlour at home, as the gig passed noiselessly over the snow-covered bridge; the happiness of passing from the cold air to the warmth and the kisses and the smiles of that familiar hearth, where the pattern of the rug and the grate and the fire-irons were 'first ideas' that it was no more possible to criticise than the solidity and extension of matter.**

This is hard writing because it requires us to *actively* participate, not simply to absorb. As modern readers, we generally read too fast: but here you need to read as you would in a book of scientific thinking, Freud or Darwin. You need to concentrate and slow down and come alive to it. Look at that seamless passing from a child's reported experience, 'seeing the bright light... the snow-covered bridge... warmth and kisses' to the complicated thought about the nature of a child's experience:

> **the pattern of the rug and the grate and the fire-irons were 'first ideas' that it was no more possible to criticise than the solidity and extension of matter.**

If you don't actively follow these words as you read, you will soon be lost. From the description of Tom loving being home, George Eliot brings in a hypothetical general law of human being: what surrounds us in early childhood sets a pattern which lasts into adult life. We may choose other rugs, other fire-irons when we are older, but *we* are built up out of the feelings that we attached to those early objects and experiences of our childhood:

> **There is no sense of ease like the ease we felt in those scenes where we were born, where objects became dear to us before we had known the labour of choice, and where the outer world seemed only an extension of our own personality; we accepted and loved it as we accepted our own sense of existence and our own limbs ... And there is no better reason for preferring this (particular thing) than that it stirs an early memory; that it is no novelty in my life, speaking to me merely through my**

**present sensibilities to form and color, but the long compan-
ion of my existence, that wove itself into my joys when joys
were vivid.**

There is wonderful sense of what contemporary thinkers would call
'wellbeing' here: a sense of a unified life where feelings and objects and
time are bound together in one person, through joy. I would never choose
to buy these cauldrons in a shop. They do not speak to me 'through my
present sensibilities to form and color'; they are not my style. I love
them partly because they are mixed with memories of my grandparents,
of the fire, and the toast and their love, of things I felt when my joys
'were vivid'. They give me that elusive thing: wellbeing.

I am now the grandmother who has these cauldrons on her mantelpiece. My grandson (two years, nine months) is in the bath playing with
a plastic tea-set. This is a creative experimental process and Leo is full
of earnest concentration as he tries to float the cups and fill them with
water, as he watches the water pass effortlessly through a sieve but less
effortlessly through a small colander. His favourite word at the moment
is 'more!' He wants things repeated *ad infinitum* because he needs to see
them many times in order to establish them as realities, strong possibili-
ties, likelihoods in his mind. This is a sort of scientific enquiry.

But it is time to get out. The water is getting cold, his fingers are
beginning to shrivel, and the adults want to eat supper in adult peace,
after he has gone to bed. None of that matters to Leo. When I suggest
'out' he's still enjoying this fabulous experiment. He cries out in frustration and distress, 'Not yet! Not yet!'

'Not yet' is a language spell that allows him to hold back the reality
principle for a moment and continue what he is doing – and sometimes
it works. But not now: our needs are more pressing; we want to eat.

He's furious when I lift him out, screams 'Not yet! Not yet!' over and
over and finally subsides into body-racking sobs as his mother and I rub
him down and get his pyjamas on. When we are in the bedroom, I offer
a story and the sobs stop: suddenly everything is different.

We open the book. It's one of Jan Pienkowski's Meg and Mog stories.
The witch and her cat are making a spell but something is going terribly
wrong. There are explosions. 'Where's Mog?' I ask him and he points
to the cat. 'Where's the cauldron?' Leo points to the cauldron. 'What's
Meg putting in the cauldron?' I ask him and he recites the list of spell
ingredients. He is altogether caught up in the discovered world.

In the bath-experiment, Leo was actively manipulating objects and
forces – water, gravity, plastic. While part of his intelligence was involved
in creating the experiment, part was engaged in observing it and another
part in thinking about it. But with the book there is nothing for him to do
physically, the concentration is total: all his energy goes into the observ-

ing and thinking about what he is observing. The book it is all here: the pictures and words present a created universe with experiments going on (as in George Eliot). What we have to do – our part – is to observe, meditate, reflect. Well, dear reader, Leo in the bath is a model of a person living a life in the world. You are busy. Things happen, you try to work them out, a lot's happening at once, some of it incomprehensible. Only part of your mind can ever be on the experience because most of your mind is doing, making, acting. And without the thinking, meditative self it is finally just chaos: we must think.

The book is a selective, ordered model of reality. It is easier to see here: things slow down; we can concentrate on one thing at a time. This may be the key aspect of reading and the reason that the Get Into Reading read-aloud model (books read aloud slowly over time in a group) is so powerful. It allows us to be here *now*, to keep a concentrated mindfulness going. If I were reading *Middlemarch* in a Get Into Reading group with other concentrated people, I would be getting a lot more out of it than I am on my sleepy own late at night.

The next day when we are lighting the fire, Leo looks up and sees one of the brass cauldrons – notices it for what must be the first time.

'Cauldron?' he says, as if to himself.

'Cauldron,' he says again as if checking the brass reality with his mental image from the last night's book. Then again, more confidently, he asserts: 'Cauldron.' reaching for it now. I observe his fingers touch the serrated edge.

What Leo has done: read a book, thought about it deeply, not really understood it all (because he did not know what a cauldron was in actuality) but he has got from that experience a template, a shape, a map, a set of pointers about life. Going back into life, he is able to recognise something he learned in the book (cauldron). He has been a creative reader and he has experienced a bigger reality because of the book. This is exactly what is happening, albeit in a more complex way, to me as I read George Eliot. That section about Tom coming home in *The Mill on the Floss* cleared a space in me and filled it with a thought-shape which was later filled out by Leo and cauldron. Books go forwards into our experience as well as backwards: they anticipate things you might know or understand later as well as things you know now, which is why we should all read books that are too hard or too old for us sometimes.

The New Economics Foundation has formulated 5 Ways to Wellbeing. One of them is 'Take Notice'. Books build our capacity to do that. I must make more time for reading.

http://reachingout.thereader.org.uk/get-into-reading.html
http://www.neweconomics.org/projects/five-ways-well-being
http://www.skyarts.co.uk/video/video-jan-pienkowski-on-the-book-show/

YOUR REGULARS

OR WE DIE

Enid Stubin

n mid-January we make good our escape from the holidays, that two-month maelstrom of obligation, panic, and excess. For academics, the timing coincides with final exams and papers and the attendant anxieties of grading, along with the cheerless run of parties. I always find myself in some chain store with the sense that I've forgotten something for somebody.

As a restorative from the season of Mylar bags for wine, the metallic-laced ribbons, and scented candles, a friend suggested the first thirty-three lines of *Endymion*. I kept shtum about the fact that I couldn't quite place them: it had been a long time since I'd read any Keats. Opening Miriam Allott's edition, my graduate school textbook, I was astonished by the quiet assurance of that opening to *A Poetic Romance*: a meditation on the pleasures of this earth that yields nothing to loss. 'A thing of beauty is a joy forever: / Its loveliness increases; it will never / Pass into nothingness; but still will keep / A bower quiet for us, and a sleep / Full of sweet dreams, and health, and quiet breathing.' The poignancy of that assertion is breath*taking* – we need to set aside our knowledge of the poet's own unquiet breathing, his tortured gasps at the end of that brief, dazzling life, and consider his startling equation of beauty and life itself. The things of this world – Keats enlists nature in the creation of a gorgeous catalog that serves as a stay against death. How the 'dooms / We have imagined for the mighty dead' manage to evoke a 'cheering light' that sustains us is no mere trick of the mind but a tenet of faith. These 'essences' establish our very being: 'They always must be with us, or we die.'

Teaching poetry in an undergraduate survey class tests these beliefs. My students have trouble with the closing couplet of Shakespeare's Sonnet 18: 'So long as men can breathe, or eyes can see, / So long lives this, and this gives life to thee.' Despite the helpful question 'For Analysis' in our weighty anthology ('What is "this" in line 14?') and some lively class discussion that revealed the 'right' answer as 'the poem itself,' at the final exam, very few got the notion of 'this' as the enduring artifact before us. Instead, 'this' became versions of 'his lady love's beauty' or 'the love they shared together,' and, crestfallen, I ticked off points for Part I ('Identify the work and author and write a sentence or two on the significance of the quote to the entire work'). But the couplet may have reached beyond corporeality: not merely the 'thisness' of the fourteen lines but a realm of imagination and fulfillment summoned by the poet's voice. Sarah Coley wonders if, far from not 'getting' it, my students are affected more deeply than I know by the sonnet, 'as if it has done its work already and given that life to "thee" and beauty.' Reading Shakespeare through Keats – could I have asked my class for anything better?

Years before first entering *Endymion*'s green world, I'd read the American poet Sara Teasdale in an anthology more primitive and less didactic that the one I would assign to English 30 D01E: 'Spend all you can on loveliness / Buy it, and never count the cost.' At the time it came across as an indulgent invitation to shop, and Keats's 'thing of beauty' appears to elevate the material until we grow up a little or a lot. The disappearance of a favorite pen (Anne Frank's entry in her diary engages us completely), misplaced sunglasses, a scarf gone astray – how much of childhood is defined by the acquisition or loss of things? And does this getting and spending reveal our materialism or a deeper response to absence? In 'One Art,' Elizabeth Bishop's speaker assures us that 'The art of losing isn't hard to master,' suggesting that one begin with 'the fluster / of lost door keys' and ascend – or fall – to the relinquishment of a lover. In the final stanza, the speaker's hand interrupts the line – '(*Write* it!)' – and exposes the pain the poem was attempting to mediate. Surrounded by stuff and people, we find more of them attaching to and defining us, and that's the signal for the organizing experts to pare away the excess, reduce our clutter, box up our memories in tidier closets.

Enmired and muddled but determined to make my grungy flat hospitable, I spent the year's end in a tsunami of scouring and purging, and the thinginess of decades oppressed me mightily. 'Can you get rid of this stuff?' Paula asked me as she deftly wielded a broom she'd made me buy that morning. No: the grotesque cut-glass vase, a tureen in the shape of a hen, and crazed ceramic candlesticks all had to be displayed for the benefit of their donors, my guests. Not only a technician of cleaning but a sagacious soul as well, Paula stacked CDs in baskets bought for another purpose, tucked wayward paperbacks into interstices she found among the shelves, and announced, 'I'm throwing away the postcards and keeping the photos.' *Ça va* by me, I thought, and after eleven hours of our joint effort reveled in the gleaming floors and polished surfaces. The postcards may have been expunged, but boxes of letters were dusted off, their contents safe. One of them held a note sent me back in the 1990s, in IBM Selectric typescript – you'd know it as Courier font. In it, Susan remembered despondent early-spring days, gray and wet, when Larry would look at her and say pointedly, 'You need Dickens.' *You need* – not a drink, a night's sleep, or a course of psychotherapy, but Dickens. Imagine that prescription – I can't remember ever feeling so envious or admiring of someone for such intuitive, compassionate, and somehow rigorous counsel at hand.

Twenty years later, our fantasies of the good life, debased versions of Keatsian luxuries, have curdled. The banks have all but collapsed, nevertheless managing to reward their officers with bloated bonuses. Haiti *has* collapsed. In the local news stories given to the rescue efforts, returning cops and firefighters marvel at the people's spirit. Accustomed to sponsoring blockbuster holiday gift drives at home, they mention, voices breaking, that even in those poor homes left intact by the earthquake, they saw no toys. I was hoping for some word from Edwidge Danticat, daughter of Haiti, and within a week a spare and haunting piece appeared in *The New Yorker*. But it's her stories in *Krik? Krak!* and *The Farming of Bones* that I might have turned to for comfort, for wisdom, for her luminous, searing portraits of endurance.

We need Dickens – ah, yes, and more than ever. Dickens and Shakespeare and Keats, Chekhov and Mahfouz and Danticat for their language and light, for their words that appear in such a way, as a splendid teacher and scholar once said, that one never wishes to change them. These writers and their writing, 'bound to us so fast / That, whether there be shine or gloom o'ercast, / They always must be with us, or we die.'

YOUR REGULARS

THE LONDON EYE
PANTOMIME SEASON

ajor spaces on the London Underground cur-
rently advertise Jeremy Clarkson's original
opinion: 'Shakespeare? I'd rather stick pencils
in my eyes!' The truculent and crumpled/
boyish face of Jeremy peeps out from the cover
of the new book featured alongside this latest witticism, but no, he isn't
wearing a school cap and blowing a raspberry. And furthermore, his
publishers treat his views with remarkable respect, pronouncing his
new book 'fearless' and 'independent'.

Jeremy Clarkson is published by Penguin. In its recent round-up of
the decade's 'Literary Heroes and Villains', the *Independent* demanded to
know what the Penguin brand, most associated with classics, thought
it was doing in projecting this altogether anti-literary, anti-canon, anti-
respect-for-your-betters point of view across the Tube. A fair question
– or is it?

One got the sense, reading this article in the *Independent* (published
18/12/09 and still available online if you want to read it for yourself)
that its writer was generally suspicious of the two-facedness of the large
publishing houses, who can spoon-feed Dan Brown, Clarkson or celebrity memoirs to an open-mouthed public, while at the same time serving
up Booker prize-winners and offering to guard the nation's literary her-
itage. Gail Rebuck, CEO of Random House, is cast as a Literary Villain,
and comes in for some particularly acidic jibes; the only real accusation
seeming to be that she runs a modern, corporate company. Corporate

companies, like lawyers, bankers and other money-makers, can be so easily substituted for the word 'evil' in most vocabularies. It is therefore distasteful to our *Independent* journalist that the corporate Random House should put their mucky paws all over 'literature'. They should stick to reaping profits from celebrity memoirs, and while they're at it, allow struggling small literary imprints to go ahead and fail, quietly and respectably, instead of buying them up and forcing them into profitable shape. Meanwhile, the article proceeds, the Independent Alliance flies the flag for 'editorial excellence, diverse publishing, innovation in marketing and commercial success' (qualities that big corporate publishers are presumed to snigger at). This group of publishers include Canongate, Faber & Faber and Quercus, to name a few of the saving graces of our industry. These Literary Heroes would turn their noses up, it is implied, at Russell Brand's *Booky Wook*, even if they had the money to pay his advance.

December is the month for pantomimes, and perhaps I should not have expected in-depth journalism in an article which was essentially a parade of effigies at which to boo and cheer. However, as I work for a large publishing company, and have absolutely nothing to do with celebrity memoirs, I know how wide of the mark this piece was, and which temporising details the writer chose to omit.

Corporate publishing houses can turn out good books in great numbers, despite or even *because* of the fact that they turn out 'bad books' in even greater numbers. The profits Jeremy Clarkson brings in for Penguin will fund the publication of a number of obscure classics somewhere down the line, or another of their consistently innovative Classics marketing initiatives. In 2008, the winners of the Booker, Costa, and Orange prizes were all published by imprints at none other than the dastardly Random House.

As the BBC drearily pointed out during their coverage of 2009's Booker ceremony in October, sales of even these prize-winning titles are not enough to keep the book industry ticking over. Clap and whistle then for Harry Potter (an *Independent* Literary Hero) who won over millions to reading despite the glitzier charms of internet, television and gaming. Stomp your feet too, surely, for Stephenie Meyer whose writing needn't make Martine McCutcheon blush, but her Twilight books are outselling the boy-wizard and even turning teenagers on to Emily Bronte (canny HarperCollins recently published a sympathetically-designed *Wuthering Heights* complete with sticker declaring 'Bella and Edward's favourite book'). While we're at it, put your hands together for James Patterson, who may not even write all his own books but is the most borrowed author from beleaguered British libraries. And here the lines between good books and commercial success begin to blur, as the commercially successful titles make the publication of their neglected but finer quality counterparts possible; as necessary an evil as the Ugly Sisters in the story of Cinderella.

The feel of the book in the hand, the interest in turning the page, even if those pages are badly written trash, that's *something*. That feel of the book in the hand may start the reader off in an interest that will lead her or him to other kinds of book that the *Independent* and *The Reader* and the publishing houses would respect more. And those better books are being written and found, and they are being published.

Here's where the writer of the *Independent* article should have flung his darts. There is still room for all kinds of books, good and bad, in publishing houses both corporate and independent, but this diversity is not reflected when it comes to actually *selling* those books. When the curtain finally fell on Borders before Christmas, the high street was left entirely to Waterstone's and their centralised buyers. We can't look for diversity of choice from W. H. Smiths – it's barely a bookshop any longer, selling only the bestsellers, and those in limited promotions, and they charge publishers a pretty penny for the pleasure. The same goes for the supermarkets, increasingly dominant, huge and flat-footed monsters firmly planted on the field of bookselling, whom we must rely on to sell a handful of titles in big numbers.

All unseasonably grim stuff, so I'm grateful for all signs that the lack of independence, or independents, in bookselling isn't stifling everybody. While changing trains on the Tube the other day, I noticed with glee that some graffiti artist had taken a pen to one of Jeremy Clarkson's ubiquitous adverts, and obligingly drawn in the pencils. Out, vile jelly! Three cheers for pro-Shakespeare rebel antics on the underground.

YOUR REGULARS

ASK THE READER

Brian Nellist

Q We seem today to be surrounded by voices uttering competing and aggressive rationalities in the languages of economics, sociology and the natural sciences. Surely *The Reader* must agree with me that like John Stuart Mill, exhausted by this aridity we must look to literature to offer instead the voice of feeling. For him it was the great Romantics. At this bitter end of the Enlightenment we can find no joy in the coolly complacent claim that great literature simply expresses 'what oft was thought but ne'er so well expressed'.

A That voice of feeling can I fear be just as imperialist as the harsh tones of reason. The distinction itself can too readily become just another version of the old body and soul dichotomy in which the one extreme produces the other. Literature I would hope has always been the ground where to think is also to feel and feeling inevitably becomes reflection. One reason why it so often produces imagery, metaphors, the interrelating of physical and mental, whatever you want to call it, is not simply to clarify and elucidate thought, if often doesn't, but to find thought within a range of feelings personal to the writer. That line of Pope from his *Essay on Criticism* with which you close your question is actually a case in point. It is part of an argument (which has always belonged in poetry as well as in prose discourse) that the writer must respect 'nature', not unlike what later writers would describe as reality. He criticises a tendency to purely intellectual display, a self-conscious delight in the intricacies of expression for their own sake, a constant danger when the process of writing becomes its own end and he uses the metaphor of dress. The writer clothes the world in words and shows his respect for the form of things, for the underlying truth, a pertinent image at a time when extravagant clothing could distort the human shape. In the line you object to, it is not the division between thought and expression you should attend to but that little word 'ne'er'. The line honours what is too often thought of as a purely Romantic concept, originality. Often, I know, when reading I will be shocked into recognition, 'Yes, that's it. That's what I think (or feel, or sense, or partly know). Only, I hadn't realised it before'. Exactness is not a purely mental agreement but a source of joy and sudden serenity which touches the whole mind.

The danger in your question lies, I suggest, in allowing categories originally intended to help us make distinctions to become (as Humpty Dumpty would say to Alice) 'our masters'. In our simplified model of cultural history the strenuousness of the Renaissance is followed by the rational calm of the Enlightenment, from which Romanticism liberates the feelings to revolutionary fervour. But in its English origins with the Cambridge Platonists, Enlightenment was a religious concept, a derivative from the old reverence for 'Right Reason' not analytical thinking. Benjamin Whichcote, for example, writes 'Man is sure of nothing; he is not sure of himself. Man is a wonder to himself' and answers in a later thought 'The spirit of man is the candle of the Lord; lighted by God and lighting us to God'. That image of the candle lies behind the phrase of Swift which so moved Matthew Arnold 'sweetness and light'. In Swift's *Battle of the Books* a spider points to his web as a mastery of design founded on his modern skills in architecture and mathematics but the bee defends her own existence by pleading that she offers man 'the two noblest of things, which are sweetness and light', honey and wax candles. Just because they were so conscious of the surrounding darkness ('Man is sure of nothing'), such writers valued its clarification even by so feeble a light as a candle. In the great series of antitheses that open the second part of Pope's *Essay on Man* he describes our condition:

A being darkly wise and rudely great:
With too much knowledge for the Sceptic side,
With too much weakness for the Stoic's pride,
He hangs between.

That final half line forces us to look back at the oxymoron, the impossible contradiction, with which we live. 'Enlightenment', if we are going to use the term, has as complex a series of meanings as 'Romanticism' itself.

Too often what you term 'aggressive rationalities' are unsatisfactory not because they ignore feeling – they don't, as 'aggressive' implies – but because they betray thought itself. 'Conceptual' is a term used currently

DAWN POTTER

ON JUNK AND THE COMMON READER

WOOLF, DU MAURIER AND BALDWIN

Dawn Potter

I submitted an essay to a journal that had previously published two of my essays. In response I received an affectionate rejection letter from the editor. The essay, she said regretfully, had 'too much different stuff going on' and the mess was 'pulling it apart.'

In addition to valuing this editor's acumen, I serve as my own dissatisfied critic, perpetually carping about my abilities and motivations and fussing over my intellectual instability. Thus, though I was melancholic, I saw no reason to disbelieve the editor. Yet as I lay in bed that night wondering what I might do with my thirteen pages of unpublishable manuscript, I found myself returning again and again to the problem of 'too much different stuff' – if problem it was: because the more I thought about the editor's difficulty with the piece, the more I realised that the heart of the trouble lay in my avoidance of the stuff issue.

My grandfather was a more traditional packrat, a careful saver of almost every item that passed through his hands, the kind of collector who conscientiously stacked fifty years' worth of foam meat trays and Ken-L Ration cans in his back shed just in case they might come in handy. And every once in a while, they did come in handy. Nonetheless, after he died, my mother was left with an untenable mess on her hands – an accumulation not just of cans and meat trays but also of hundreds of neatly folded diocese newspapers that no one had ever dreamed of reading; twenty-five or thirty threadbare work jackets crowded onto five or ten coat hooks; four outbuildings and a two-story house overflowing with broken 1920s-era farm equipment, chipped enamel dishpans, three-legged chairs, and several generations of mouse nests; a dozen Maxwell House cans filled with a remarkable number of nickels; and an accumulation of baling twine from several thousand hay bales – a mountainous headache in itself, which was exacerbated by the discovery that he had also secreted a considerable amount of cash in and among these various collections.

Like my dear inscrutable grandfather, I am also a packrat, though I am not tempted to hoard ancient supermarket trays or empty rusty cans. What I can't throw out is my reading clutter. Take this week, for instance. Thanks to the disorganised and unpredictable Fate who weaves my book trajectory, I happened to be bobbing between two story collections at the same time: James Baldwin's *Going to Meet the Man*, which compiles stories from the 1940s through the 1960s; and Daphne du Maurier's *Don't Look Now*, a new selection of stories that were originally published during the same era. I had received an open-ended invitation from the aforementioned editor to write about the du Maurier collection, but by chance had recently acquired a remaindered copy of Baldwin's stories at Marden's, a strange Maine store that was also selling end tables in the shape of Sammy Davis, Jr.

Being on assignment, I aspired to brisk, intelligent coherence. But as one might expect, the collections are very different from one another, so different that I briefly wondered if brevity and date of composition might be their only common traits. Meanwhile, I continued to read – slouched on the sofa with a large poodle wedged uncomfortably between my feet, coiled over cheese and crackers at the kitchen table, or shivering in the car as I waited for my son's late bus to roar into the school parking lot – and I found myself alternating between the volumes with a growing curiosity about how and why writers seem to gravitate, almost against their will, to specific techniques and emphases and how those authorial susceptibilities influence the way in which a reader ends up classifying the work. In other words, I got distracted: a fissure opened in my attention; and, as generally happens, that crack began admitting scraps and dust and unidentifiable fluid impressions from the books that are stacked like foam meat trays in the back shed of my brain.

Samuel Taylor Coleridge is cranky about readers such as myself,

A comprehensive class characterized by reconciling the two contrary yet co-existing propensities of human nature, namely, indulgence of sloth, and hatred of vacancy. In addition to novels and tales of chivalry in prose or rhyme, (by which last I mean neither rhythm nor metre), the genus comprises as its species, gaming, swinging or swaying on a chair or gate; spitting over a bridge; smoking; snuff-taking; tête-à-tête quarrels after dinner between husband and wife; conning word by word all the advertisements of a daily newspaper in a public house on a rainy day, &c. &c. &c.

Yet as Virginia Woolf admitted in her essay 'Pure English,' 'an irrational element enters into [readers'] liking and disliking of books as certainly as it enters into their feelings for people.' In other words, why *can't* a committed reader also enjoy swaying on a gate and spitting over a bridge? I daresay Coleridge conned newspaper advertisements in more than one pub over the course of his life, not to mention played the leading part in a number of quarrels after dinner. But for collectors, wrestling with irrationality is not our only trouble. Somehow, as one accumulates more and more items, the individual pieces begin to sort themselves into multiple and anomalous groupings. Everything influences everything else. So as I sat on the couch reading du Maurier's and Baldwin's stories, I was reading, in a way, not only the books I had open on my lap but all the crumpled, dog-eared stories piled in my head. Like the bent ploughshares and crushed peach baskets cluttering my grandfather's chicken house, that literary scrap heap does come in handy now and again. But it can also create an untenable mess: which brings me back to the essay I submitted to my friendly, long-suffering editor.

In a way, the Baldwin and du Maurier could serve as symbols for the mixed-up role that reading plays in my life. I am Baldwinesque in that I take reading seriously. For example, I have no patience with people who tell me they read to relax. Relaxation is practically the furthest thing from my mind. I am a tense, ambitious, and greedy reader, and I don't want to be lulled; I want to be swallowed up. On the other hand, I am du Maurien insofar as I am democratic about what I choose to read. In other words, if I have a taste for the classics, I also have a taste for trash. Coleridge would not be surprised to learn, for instance, about my louche affection for nineteenth-century women's pulp fiction, such as the forgotten bestsellers of Mrs. E.D.E.N. Southworth (author of, among innumerable others, the alluringly titled *A Beautiful Fiend*), not to mention the novels of Mary J. Holmes, whose Millbank I found in my grandfather's aforementioned house of junk when I was ten years old and which I have since reread at least once a year for more than thirty years.

Now my attention, for reasons best known to itself, had begun to wander into the hazy realm of the trash novel, leaving me haplessly affixing pseudo-connectives between du Maurier and Southworth, who soon morphed unexpectedly into novelist and essayist John Fowles. 'It was Fowles,' I scribbled (what is the word for scribbling with a laptop?), 'who wrote somewhere that bad novels are a key to their times. Like "real literature" these books fill some hole in me; they help me understand what it means to be alive. Even though they are not art, they manage, in spite of themselves, to occasionally achieve the goals of art.'

Downstairs, the parakeet squawked, and my husband's radio emitted distracting and uncongenial tunes. I hunched over my desk and wrote: 'I don't for a moment believe that E.D.E.N. Southworth's novels rival George Eliot's or Emily Brontë's.' (Damn. Where did Eliot and Brontë come from?) 'Yet in her books I glimpse a particular portrait of the age – a focus, for instance, on the petty sexual distractions of its women – that I don't necessarily see in Eliot's or Brontë's work but that gives me a new angle of vision and thus broadens my comprehensions and my sympathies.'

I blathered on about Southworth for a while longer, evoking her flabby plots, her stock characters, her stilted purple prose, comparing her along the way to both the Steve Miller Band and Velveeta. I dredged up a fake memory of kissing a boy under the bleachers and a real one of eating a grilled-cheese sandwich, then suddenly ended a paragraph with the Romantic realisation that 'Nobody else is me', at which point the long-suffering editor must have said, 'Thank God'. Finally, after much shuffling, I found my way back to Daphne du Maurier, pointing out that her stories may be gothic, formulaic potboilers (my grasp at making Southworth relevant) but are also carefully, often exquisitely, crafted. Always she maintains a clean, efficient control of plot, and her settings are so vividly evoked that even familiar, rather dull places can seem feverishly surreal, as in this scene from the story 'Split Second':

> **She walked swiftly past the nurses pushing prams, two or three of them in groups chatting together, their charges running ahead. Dogs barked beside the ponds. Solitary men in mackintoshes stared into vacancy. An old woman on a seat threw crumbs to chirping sparrows. The sky took on a darker, olive tone. Mrs. Ellis quickened her steps. The fairground by the Vale of Health looked sombre, the merry-go-round shrouded in its winter wrappings of canvas, and two lean cats stalked each other in and out of the palings. A milkman, whistling, clanked his tray of bottles and, lifting them to his cart, urged the pony to a trot.**

There is something altogether beautiful about that passage – a combined effect of its rhythmic sentence construction and the author's swift, subtle control of her reader's eye, moving attention from earth to sky, from near to far, from human to animal. Yes, certainly, du Maurier is not in Mrs. E.D.E.N. Southworth's class, where beauty is reduced to striking 'at first sight with an electric thrill.' But as I suddenly verified in the course of my scuffling writing project, she is just as certainly not in James Baldwin's class. I may not like all of the stories in Baldwin's *Going to Meet the Man*, but my discomfort is primarily a personal reaction to his protagonists' cursory cruelty. It has nothing to do with the intensely character-driven energy of his writing, as in 'The Outing,' in which even the minor players cohere into furious, vibrating personalities:

> **Last year Sister McCandless had held an impromptu service in the unbelieving subway car she played the tambourine and sang and exhorted sinners and passed through the train distributing tracts. Not everyone [in the church] had found this admirable, to some it seemed that Sister McCandless was being a little ostentatious. 'I praise my Redeemer wherever I go,' she retorted defiantly. 'Holy Ghost don't leave me when I leave the church. I got a every day religion.'**

Baldwin is a ferocious writer, very nearly eviscerating himself in his relentless imaginative quest to link vision and word, though he may speak only of a church picnic or a slow evening in a nightclub. Du Maurier, on the other hand, composes plot after horror-packed plot; yet her authorial voice remains detached, almost indifferent. Reading 'The Birds' (which Alfred Hitchcock transformed into a movie I'm too scared to watch but that du Maurier is said to have disliked), I find her dry, ruthless narration far more unnerving than the situation she describes:

> **As [Nat] jumped the stile he heard the whirr of wings. A black-backed gull dived down at him from the sky, missed, swerved in flight, and rose to dive again. In a moment it was joined by others, six, seven, a dozen, black-backed and herring mixed. Nat dropped his hoe. The hoe was useless. Covering his head with his arms he ran towards the cottage. They kept coming at him from the air, silent save for the beating wings. The terrible, fluttering wings. He could feel the blood on his hands, his wrists, his neck. Each stab of a swooping beak tore his flesh. If only he could keep them from his eyes. Nothing else mattered. He must keep them from his eyes.**

It's so difficult, in that passage, to care about what happens to Nat. Like the rest of the humans in the story, he functions simply as an obstacle to bird domination, although he is a larger obstacle than most. Clearly the author herself was far more interested in the gulls than in Nat's survival; and even as she describes their actions, I sense her dispassion. She is on a remote hillside, studying the flock through her binoculars and taking tidy, careful notes.

Baldwin, in contrast, hurls himself into the fray:

> **'Well, glory!' cried Father James. The Holy Ghost touched him and he cried again, 'Well, bless Him! Bless his holy name!' [The congregation] laughed and shouted after him, their joy so great that they laughed as children and some of them cried as children do; in the fullness and assurance of salvation,**

in the knowledge that the Lord was in their midst and that each heart, swollen to anguish, yearned only to be filled with His glory. Then, in that moment, each of them might have mounted with wings like eagles far past the sordid persistence of the flesh, the depthless iniquity of the heart, the doom of hours and days and weeks; to be received by the Bridegroom where He waited on high in glory; where all tears were wiped away and death had no power; where the wicked ceased from troubling and the weary soul found rest.

The various side-issues and interfering tangents that clotted my original essay helped me to find this thought. Apparently, for whatever reason, my intellectual growth seems to require a certain amount of meandering through my mental library. But I realise as I write these words that I have absolutely no inkling how other people figure out what they think. Does anyone else require such a galaxy of literary advisers? I'm not talking about research but about grasping wildly at straws.

Virginia Woolf in 'Character in Fiction' writes 'Novelists differ from the rest of the world because they do not cease to be interested in character when they have learnt enough about it for practical purposes':

When all the practical business of life has been discharged, there is something about people which continues to seem to them of overwhelming importance, in spite of the fact that it has no bearing whatever upon their happiness, comfort, or income. The study of character becomes to them an absorbing pursuit; to impart character an obsession. And this I find very difficult to explain: what novelists mean when they talk about character, what the impulse is that urges them so powerfully every now and then to embody their view in writing.

I was delighted when Woolf leaped so cogently into my essay, but the journal editor took pointed exception to the intrusion: 'Woolf turns out to be too heavily woven into the fabric... and she is a mistake. She is not always a mistake, but here she is pulling you too far astray, into her thoughts, when what you want to be doing is having your own.' This was rather crushing, for I'd assumed I had been having my own thoughts. Yet if these unexpected collisions weren't thinking, then what could thinking be? Despite the journal editor's distaste for her interference, Woolf's presence in my essay gave me some clue as to why an *ought* can be so influential. Toward the end of 'Character in Fiction,' she points her exculpatory finger at readers who 'allow the writers to palm off upon you a version of [character], which has no likeness to that surprising apparition whatsoever':

In your modesty you seem to consider that writers are of different blood and bone from yourselves... Never was there a more fatal mistake. It is this division between reader and writer, this humility on your part, these professional airs and graces on ours, that corrupt and emasculate the books which should be the healthy offspring of a close and equal alliance between us. Hence spring those sleek, smooth novels, those portentous and ridiculous biographies, that milk and watery criticism, those poems melodiously celebrating the innocence of roses and sheep which pass so plausibly for literature at the present time.

Woolf is such a good writer, and such a literary patrician, that I almost always humbly go along with whatever she says. But as she herself points out, a reader's humility gives a writer too much leeway for laziness or error; and in Woolf's case, my humility makes it too easy for her get away with deriding entire genres and styles that don't happen to suit her taste. Presumably du Maurier's fiction would fall into Woolf's 'sleek, smooth' category, a generalisation that does, in fact, have some justification. Du Maurier's dialogues, for instance, feel strangely prefabricated. But when Woolf summarily dismisses the pantheon of writers who rely on such canned techniques of characterisation, she also avoids consideration of why a particular skilled and careful writer might continue to depend on them. And in du Maurier's case, the choice seems to illustrate how easily we readers and writers *learn* to discount individual suffering in our pursuit of narrative thrill. Did du Maurier find herself, as a writer, trapped by that pursuit? Did she take a certain malicious or ironic pleasure in proving she could entrap her readers? Did she see her stories as efforts to prove the existence of a terrible immorality? Although such questions may be unanswerable, I think there is no doubt that she was conscious of her methods, if not her motives.

The journal editor saw my excursion into Woolf as a distraction, as indeed it was. Yet if VW had not made her unexpected appearance, I would not have had a chance to puzzle over her assertions and, to my surprise, find myself defending du Maurier, whose books I don't particularly admire. This process may not be thought per se, but it is a shift in perspective, a way to look at a piece of art more carefully, with a more perplexed vision.

Not long ago, I rented Leni Riefenstahl's propaganda film *Triumph of the Will*, which documents the Third Reich's 1934 party rally at Nuremberg. As I sat on my couch, drinking tea and watching platoon after platoon of young Germans, old Germans, soldiers, working people, farmers, and flower-decked maidens march past Riefenstahl's lens, I realised suddenly and viscerally that evil is everywhere, crouching and invisible, infiltrating the air I was breathing, like a spore or a virus. No one is immune. Everyone is vulnerable. And I realised also that the books I was reading were contemporaneous with these horrors. Du Maurier composed her stories alongside them; and in their chill tone and meaningless cruelty, her stories parallel their times. Woolf, too, lived in that era, as did Baldwin. Yet each artist, despite an overlapping history, dealt with characterisation personally and idiosyncratically; each struggled with habits and predilections and avoidances and fears. Art, like history, like love, is confused and complicated.

At the end of 'Sonny's Blues,' probably James Baldwin's most famous short story, the narrator recalls the night he went to a jazz club and, for the first time, heard his younger brother Sonny play the piano.

'All I know about music, is that not many people ever really hear it. And even then, on the rare occasions when something opens within, and the music enters, what we mainly hear, or hear corroborated, are personal, private, vanishing evocations. But the man who creates the music is hearing something else, is dealing with the roar rising from the void and imposing order on it as it hits the air.'

My essay on du Maurier and Baldwin has now melted away into thin air. But if nothing else, my back-shed bits and scraps of cultural memory cohere as a 'personal, private, vanishing evocation.' The jumble is clutter, but it speaks to me, teaches me, comforts me. It defines my individuality as a common reader, to borrow yet again from Woolf. Yet as I glance at her brief essay 'The Common Reader,' I remember that she herself has borrowed the phrase from Samuel Johnson:

The common reader, as Dr. Johnson implies, differs from the critic and the scholar. He is worse educated, and nature has not gifted him so generously... Above all, he is guided by an instinct to create for himself, out of whatever odds and ends he can come by, some kind of whole... He never ceases as he reads, to run up some rickety and ramshackle fabric which shall give him the temporary satisfaction of looking sufficiently like the real object to allow of laughter, affection, and argument.

And so I think, Well, all right, Virginia. We're in the same boat then, aren't we? Which is, on some days, accomplishment enough.

FICTION

THE AFTERNOON

R. K Richey

The Late Afternoon of August 16, 1977 in Chattanooga

They used to be known as plumbers but now the side of the company truck said they were mechanical contractors. Regardless, Si still called himself a plumber because it was easier to say. When he tried saying 'mechanical contractor,' it came out of his mouth something like: *mechanic's contrack*.

Si didn't know exactly how old he was, only what he had been told: that he was born in Alabama and came up to Tennessee with his mama when he was two. In a few years from now, after he couldn't work any longer, this age question would present major problems for him with the Social Security Administration. He couldn't read and write, had no papers indicating his real age, and, even though he thought he was seventy-five, he admitted to the case worker then that he could have been closer to eighty because he knew he went to work as a plumber's helper at age ten in 1911 or 1912 (or so he was told). There hadn't been a day of school, ever. No military.

THE READER CROSSWORD

Cassandra No.29

ACROSS

1. Lost for words in front of Cenotaph as icy wind blows (7)
5. Odious fault he amended (7)
9. Former currency in disenfranchised state (5)
10. Robin's harbinger of snow? (9)
11. Should work on this presumably before 21 across (2, 12)
13. Where and what to drink in France (4)
14. Poem delivered from the left at a brisk pace (1, 7)
17. Acentric options for North America and Greenland (8)
18. He sounds rather lazy but is often available for afternoon performances (4)
21. Putting forward plan for pressing one's suit? (6, 8)
23. Rattle produced by petite car (9)
*24. See 3 down
25. First signs of love are sighing and groaning, not eating food (7)
26. A small amount of alcohol can make the leap possible (7)

DOWN

1. Romeo's preferred form of transport? (4)
*2. Midnight hour cause of hatred for snakes perhaps (5, 2, 8)
*3 and 24 across. Bond salesman undercover (6, 5)
*4. See 19 down
5. Scold these two chaps soundly (8)
6. The nodal signs are too hot for this (2, 6)
7. Responsibility for RE in favour of the one holding the baby (3, 3, 9)
8. Songs not too good when the bird is off colour (4, 6)
12. Prudent conversion of ice cool man (10)
15. Detecting the spreading of fragrance (8)
16. Shift residence of princess (8)
*19 and 4. Around the beginning of Christmas Jordan hopes to see our writer (6, 6)
20. Trip taken in the guise of envoy, agent of state (6)
22. Return of ceramics leads to arrest (4)

*Clues with an asterisk have a common theme

124 OXFORD UNIVERSITY PRESS

BUCK'S QUIZ

SCRAMBLED BUCKS

Unscramble these nineteenth century authors and novels

1. A wild online dancer
2. A soda rhythm
3. Wherein thighs tug
4. Lemony tribe
5. A flipped divorce
6. Salaried unrest
7. A red dandilion
8. Watercress bother
9. Winos kill lice
10. Eaten within whom
11. A cut baby elk
12. Lacked richness
13. Egg is so ginger
14. Tell the streetcar
15. Only another plot

PRIZES!

The winner of the Crossword (plucked in time-honoured tradition from a hat) will receive our selection of World's Classics paperbacks, and the same to the winner of the fiendishly difficult Buck's Quiz.

Congratulations to Helen Robey from Southport who answered all questions correctly in Buck's Quiz, and to Jill Adamiecki from Nottingham who is the winner of the Crossword competition.

Please send your solutions (marked either Cassandra Crossword, or Buck's Quiz) to 19 Abercromby Square, Liverpool L69 7ZG.

ANSWERS

CASSANDRA CROSSWORD NO. 28

Across
1. Sultan 4. Tailor 9. Disc 10. Soldier, spy 11. Leamas 12. Whiplash 13. Assessors 15. Acme 16. John 17. Icelander 21. Atropine 22. Cassis 24. Solidifier 25. Alec 26. Tinker 27. People

Down
1. Smiley's 2. Locum 3. Assists 5. Acidic 6. Lord Lucan 7. Riposte 8. Flowery cleric 14. Ethiopian 16. Jetboat 18. Le Carre 19. Epicene 20. Finite 23. Sharp

BUCK'S QUIZ NO. 36

1. Charles Dickens 2. Seamus Heaney ('The Railway Children') 3. E. Nesbit *The Railway Children* 4. Hercule Poirot (*Murder on the Orient Express*) 5. 'O fat white woman whom nobody loves', Francis Cornford 6. W. H. Auden, 'Night Mail' 7. 'The Tay Bridge Disaster', William McGonagall 8. Bruno kills Haines wife (*Strangers on a Train*, Patricia Highsmith) 9. *Anna Karenina* 10. *Doctor Zhivago* 11. Elaine ('Middlesex', John Betjeman) 12. *Cranford* 13. *Trainspotting*, Irvine Welsh 14. *The Great Railway Bazaar* 15. Charles Dickens, *Dombey and Son (*Carker)

David Almond's first novel for young people, *Skellig* (1998), won the Whitbread Children's Novel of the Year and the Carnegie Medal. His graphic novel *The Savage* (2008) is The Liverpool Reads book for 2009.

Alison Brackenbury's seventh collection is *Singing in the Dark* (Carcanet, 2008). She has recently produced a chapbook of new animal poems, *Shadow*, available from www.happenstancepress.com. New poems can be read at her website: www.alisonbrackenbury.co.uk

Matt Bryden has taught EFL in Italy, Poland and the Czech Republic and plans to head to South Korea next. His first collection has been shortlisted for the Crashaw Prize.

David Constantine's most recent publications are *Nine Fathom Deep* (poems), *The Shieling* (short stories) and a translation of the second part of Goethe's *Faust*. With his wife Helen he edits *Modern Poetry in Translation*.

Thomas Corcoran is an undergraduate in Classics at Oxford, where his chief claim to fame was as the editor of a satirical magazine. He is currently spending a year studying and teaching English in Turin.

Neil Curry's *New and Selected Poems Other Rooms* was published by Enitharmon Press in 2007. Since then he has published critical studies of Alexander Pope and George Herbert.

Richard Gwyn is a poet and novelist and directs the MA in Creative Writing at Cardiff University. His new collection of prose poems, *Sad Giraffe Café*, is published by Arc in March 2010.

Katy Hooper is Special Collections Librarian at the University of Liverpool, and was Dinah Birch's editorial assistant on the 7th edition of *The Oxford Companion to English Literature* (2009).

Hanif Kureishi is a playwright, screenwriter, novelist and film-maker. Screenplays include *My Beautiful Launderette*. His first novel was *The Buddha of Suburbia* (1990 Faber). *Collected Stories* (Faber) will be published March 2010.

Patrick McGuinness was born in 1968, teaches French in Oxford, and lives in Caernarfon, North Wales. His latest book of poems, *Jilted City*, is published in March by Carcanet, and is a Poetry Book Society Recommendation. His novel, *The Last Hundred Days*, appears in March 2011.

Ian McMillan was born in 1956 and has been a freelance writer/performer / broadcaster since 1981. He presents *The Verb* on BBC Radio 3 every Friday night.

Dawn Potter is the author of two collections of poetry and a memoir. She is associate director of the Frost Place Conference on Poetry and Teaching and lives with her family in the Maine woods.

R. K. Richey lives in Mount Pleasant, South Carolina with his wife and son. His first collection of stories is entitled *Easter Stories*.

Julie-ann Rowell's pamphlet collection Convergence was a Poetry Book Society Recommendation. Her first full collection *Letters North* was published in 2008 by Brodie Press. She teaches poetry at the University of Bristol.

Michael Schmidt is Professor of Poetry at Glasgow University. He is editorial director of Carcanet Press and general editor of *PN Review*. He is a critic and literary historian. His *Collected Poems* were published by Smith/Doorstop in 2009.

Patrick Scott-Graham graduated from studying English and Latin American Studies at the University of Liverpool in 2008. He is now training to be a teacher through the University of Bath.

David Sergeant's first collection of poetry, *Talk Like Galileo*, will be published by Shearsman Books this April.

Eleanor Stanton is a GIR project worker based in Toxteth, Liverpool. When she's not absorbed in a book she can be found designing and making vintage-inspired handbags and jewellery, cooking feasts for her friends or looking out to sea.

Enid Stubin is Assistant Professor of English at Kingsborough Community College of the City University of New York and Adjunct Professor of Humanities at NY University's School of Continuing and Professional Studies.

Janet Westcott is Equal Access Librarian for Poole Libraries and a recently accredited Get into Reading Facilitator. She aims to have Get into Reading groups in all Poole's libraries.

The Reader Magazine
Subscription Information

UK (p&p free)

1 year	4 issues	£24.00
2 years	8 issues	£38.00
3 years	12 issues	£57.00

Abroad (p&p free)

1 year	4 issues	£36.00
2 years	8 issues	£57.00
3 years	12 issues	£86.00

Please make cheques payable to **The Reader Organisation** and post to The Reader, 19 Abercromby Square, University of Liverpool, L69 7ZG. Include your name and address and specify the issue with which you would like your subscription to begin.
Save 20% on 2- and 3-year subscriptions.
The easiest way to take out a subscription abroad is by using Paypal on our website: www.thereader.org.uk.

Distribution Information

Trade orders Contact Mark Chilver, Magazine Department, Central Books
email: mark@centralbooks.com
web: www.centralbooks.com
tel: 0845 458 9925   fax: 0845 458 9912
Central Books, 99 Wallis Road, London, E9 5LN

For any other queries regarding trade orders or institutional subscriptions, please contact Lee Keating in The Reader Office

email: leekeating@thereader.org.uk   tel: 0151 794 2830